Nuffield
Home Economics

TEACHERS' GUIDE
FIBRES AND FABRICS

General Editor, Nuffield Home Economics
Marie Edwards

Authors of this book
Barbara Booth
John Pomeroy

Organizers, Nuffield Home Economics 1977—81
Harry Faulkner
Sharon M. Mansell

The Nuffield-Chelsea Curriculum Trust would like to thank the following for their help:

International Institute for Cotton
International Wool Secretariat
Shirley Institute

Nuffield Home Economics

TEACHERS' GUIDE

FIBRES AND FABRICS

Published for the Nuffield-Chelsea Curriculum Trust
by Hutchinson Education

Hutchinson & Co. (Publishers) Ltd
An imprint of the Hutchinson Publishing Group
17–21 Conway Street, London W1P 6JD

Hutchinson Group (Australia) Pty Ltd
30–32 Cremorne Street, Richmond South, Victoria 3121
PO Box 151, Broadway, New South Wales 2007

Hutchinson Group (NZ) Ltd
32–34 View Road, PO Box 40–086, Glenfield, Auckland 10

Hutchinson Group (SA) (Pty) Ltd
PO Box 337, Bergvlei 2012, South Africa

First published 1983

British Library Cataloguing in Publication Data
Nuffield-Chelsea Curriculum Trust
    Fibres and fabrics.— (Nuffield home economics)
    Teachers' guide
    1. Textile fabrics
    I. Title   II. Series
    677   TS1445

ISBN 0 09 152861 5

Design and art direction by Ivan and Robin Dodd.

Diagrams by Rodney Paull, Gary Simmons, and Ian Smith.

Tables by Nina Konrad.

Printed in Great Britain by The Anchor Press Ltd
and bound by Wm Brendon & Son Ltd
both of Tiptree, Essex.

CONTENTS

CHAPTER 1 **Going shopping** PAGE 1

CHAPTER 2 **The clothes line** 11

CHAPTER 3 **Why textiles — why not plastics?** 24

CHAPTER 4 **Fibres: the first step in the line** 34

CHAPTER 5 **Producing the natural fibres** 48

CHAPTER 6 **Man imitates nature** 56

CHAPTER 7 **Comparing the fibres** 70

CHAPTER 8 **Building up to a yarn** 89

CHAPTER 9 **Building up to a fabric** 97

CHAPTER 10 **Colour** 106

CHAPTER 11 **Putting colour into practice** 113

CHAPTER 12 **It's all in the finish** 123

CHAPTER 13 **The garment takes shape** 132

CHAPTER 14 **Getting dirty** 141

CHAPTER 15 **Keep it clean** 145

Reference material 156

Useful addresses 158

Index 160

Preface

It is particularly fitting that the first major series of publications to be issued under the name of the Nuffield-Chelsea Curriculum Trust should be a new series in home economics. The Nuffield-Chelsea Curriculum Trust, founded in September 1979, arose out of the work of the Nuffield Foundation in the renewal of the curriculum in the sciences and mathematics. One of the foremost aims of this work has been to develop in pupils a realization of the applications of their classroom learning and its significance to the world of industry and everyday living. Home economics is, above all, the discipline in which the principles of natural laws can be seen most clearly and closely in their application to the needs of living.

This new Nuffield Home Economics project had its origins in a series of in-service courses organized by the Centre for Science and Mathematics Education at Chelsea College. These courses were set up for home economics teachers who asked for help in deepening and refreshing their awareness of aspects of scientific knowledge which are needed in the teaching of home economics.

From an initial survey of Nuffield science curricula it became clear that a wholly new project devoted to the subject of home economics was required. The Foundation granted the funds for establishing this project. A Consultative Committee under the chairmanship of Professor Harold Baum, Professor of Biochemistry at Chelsea College, was set up with a membership drawn from the Inspectorate and other experts in the field from universities, industry, and schools to guide the course of the project from its beginnings, through its trials, and its progress to publication.

The Trust owes a deep dept of gratitude to many institutions, groups, and individuals for advice and practical support: to the Inspectorate at the national and local levels for their encouragement and interest; to the local authority home economics advisers who have met regularly for progress reports on the project and who have played a central role in the trials of draft materials; to the teachers and pupils in schools in over twenty authorities who carried out the trials and gave us so much help and constructive criticism; to the colleges where courses have been held and whose members have played an active part in the development of the materials; to the Examination Boards who have shown an interest in the project; to Professor Baum and the members of the Consultative Committee; and to our many friends in the public and private industries, most notably Unilever which provided a grant enabling us to carry out much of the preliminary work and British Gas for their support in the dissemination of the project. To the organizers of the project, Sharon M. Mansell and Harry Faulkner, who have been responsible for the origination of all the materials, for their trials in schools, and for all the attendant business of the project in the period 1977–81, in addition to being the general editors of *The Basic Course*; to Marie Edwards, who is in charge of the dissemination of the project and who is general editor of the later materials; and to John Pomeroy and Barbara Booth the editors and authors of this book, I must specially record the thanks of the Trust. I also have the pleasure of thanking Professor Paul Black, academic adviser to the Trust, William Anderson, our publications manager, the editors Sarah Codrington, Deborah Williams, and Frank Kitson who have worked on the books, the designers and artists, and finally our colleagues in Hutchinson Education who have given us such encouragement and support during the period of origination and production of the materials.

K.W. Keohane
Chairman, The Nuffield-Chelsea Curriculum Trust.

Introduction

In *Fibres and fabrics* pupils learn textile science in a way that will be useful to them in everyday life. In our society nearly all clothes and household textiles are bought rather than made at home. The emphasis in this course is therefore on learning about the industrial processes involved in the manufacture of fabrics, and how these affect the clothes the pupils buy and wear. They are encouraged to consider the reasons why fabrics are made the way they are for different purposes. The relative importance of different criteria — aesthetics, performance, and price — for different purchases are dealt with in depth.

The book presents a sequence of work which develops progressively towards an understanding of textile science. It can be approached by any pupil at secondary level even without prior knowledge of the subject, although many may have benefited from a study of *The Basic Course*. Although this book does not give practical instruction in, for example, garment making, it is assumed that many teachers will use it in a course which does contain such work. Traditional skills have an important part to play in contributing to an understanding of this area of study as a whole. There are many opportunities for links to be made. Many teachers may wish to use only certain parts of the course. Each chapter is a self-contained unit and need not necessarily be taught in the order given. Chapters from other books in the series could be used in parallel with this one. For instance, cleaning methods are dealt with in *Fibres and fabrics*, Chapter 15 and in *People and homes*, Chapter 5. Teachers can use the materials as part of a variety of syllabuses for pupils of varying abilities including examination standard and beyond.

Through teaching *Fibres and fabrics*, links can constantly be made with pupils' work in other areas of study in Home Economics and with other subjects in the curriculum — not only science but also subjects such as economics, sociology, geography, and design. It is the aim of the Nuffield Home Economics project to show pupils how scientific concepts can be understood and applied. It is recognized that some pupils find difficulty in understanding scientific and mathematical concepts in the abstract. They may find them more comprehensible in an applied situation. Home Economics should be seen as a valuable opportunity to enhance the pupils' skills: for the able by injecting realism and application to abstract concepts, and for the less able by helping them to understand these concepts by offering them opportunity to put them into practice. In some cases lessons in textiles will run parallel or follow science lessons, so that the pupils will have the basic understanding which will help them to approach certain sections. But this is not essential. Some pupils may not yet have met some basic ideas, so these ideas are explained and illustrated in a straightforward way since it is always remembered that the function of this course is not to train scientists but rather to give an understanding of certain scientific ideas and an ability to apply them to the study of textiles.

The study of textiles is dynamic. The factual material included is not the final answer, but an expression of the current state. The techniques it describes are important because they enable topics to be examined and re-examined in the light of future developments.

In accordance with the Nuffield tradition, *Fibres and fabrics* seeks to provide an approach to education in the widest sense. In particular it seeks to inculcate an understanding and practice of a logical approach to problem-solving generally expressed as the scientific method. Theory and practice are closely linked together so that pupils can see the applications of what they are learning. The practical work is designed so that with the teacher's guidance the pupils can make discoveries for themselves, and play an active part in their own education.

The pupils' book is one of the four inter-related texts in Nuffield Home Economics prepared for the post thirteen age group. These books aim to develop the approach to Home Economics which *The Basic Course* provided for the earlier years. The four areas of study are:
Fibres and fabrics
Food science
Nutrition
People and homes.
Each area of study has a separate pupils' text and teachers' guide. A pack of worksheets and assessment cards is also available for each area.

The pupils' text
The pupils' text integrates practical and theoretical work. It is well illustrated and sets out instructions for all the experimental work. This is designed to be carried out in Home Economics or Textile rooms rather than in science laboratories. The experiments require no complex facilities such as fume cupboards, or complex apparatus or chemicals which may not be used safely in non-laboratory areas. Apparatus such as thermometers and microscopes which can easily be transported and set up are used, but Bunsen burners are not essential since gas taps are not always available where the classes will be held. This approach is not, however, indicative of simple science. The science concepts may, when required, be explained in depth.

At the end of each chapter of the pupils' text is a piece of Background reading on some aspects of the work covered. These are intended to broaden the pupils' knowledge of the wider aspects of the subject — historical, social, and international — and to expand their imaginative grasp of the jobs connected with the various topics.

The worksheets provide background information and additional investigations for the whole class or for groups within it. The use of the assessment cards is explained below.

The teachers' guide
This teachers' guide is designed to give all the support required for teaching the materials. Each chapter in the pupils' text has a corresponding chapter in the teachers' guide. Each one begins with a short introduction to the topic, time allocation, and a list of extension work suggested in the chapter and worksheets which may be useful. Each section starts with a summary of the main ideas. This is followed by notes on investigations in the pupils' text including a list of apparatus and materials required, answers to questions, and notes on illustrations. Ideas for homework and extension work are described. (References to figures in the pupils' text are given in italics. References to other areas of study are given thus: *People and homes*, Chapter 5. References to any area of study in *The Basic Course* are given thus: *The Basic Course*, Chapter 22.)

Processes and skills are noted in the margins throughout this teachers' guide. A list is given below.

1 Observing
Measuring
Estimating

2 Analysing
Classifying
Deciding criteria
Identifying causes
Interpreting graphs
Using statistics

3 Planning
Suggesting and designing tests
Suggesting hypotheses
Selecting equipment
Practical skills (dexterity and manipulation)
Reasoning logically

4 Assessing:
validity
relevant factors
accuracy
references

5 Communicating:
graphs
writing
speech
diagrams
maths

6 Applying knowledge
Assessing ideas
Evaluating results

Assessment
At the end of each chapter is a Summary Table. The concepts and skills covered by each section are listed together with possible

tasks and activities which should demonstrate the level of understanding achieved by the pupils. They are written in ascending order of difficulty and are intended to offer further opportunities for pupils to practise the associated skills. Tests can be conducted by asking for written answers, for homework, or orally working in small groups or with the whole class. They are intended to provide teachers with a formative assessment strategy. The assessment cards which are part of the package of worksheets are planned to provide ideas for summative assessment. They offer the teacher a variety of tests and projects for each chapter and will help towards effective assessment of pupils' performance. They are aimed to give flexibility in use. They could be used on an OHP or duplicated either in part or in their entirety for an end of term test or when a topic has been completed. In most cases, the pupils will require paper on which to answer the questions. The questions are varied and include objective questions, structured questions, and the use of mathematical forms. Each card includes a suggestion for a project or course work investigation. Many of the questions have no one right answer. Pupils should be encouraged to consider a range of possibilities. For this reason no answers are provided for questions on the assessment cards. This is a pattern of assessment common to the four texts in the Nuffield series which together form a complete assessment strategy for Home Economics.

CHAPTER 1

Going shopping

This chapter establishes the concept of relevance to everyday life and is therefore of critical importance in enabling pupils to understand the entire course.

Pupils start by thinking about a recent clothing or textile purchase which they have made and catalogue the reasons for the choice. From a series of apparently unrelated ideas a rational classification is made and the reasons for this are scientifically analysed and developed. Three basic factors are isolated as determinants in textile and clothing choice. The place of science and technology in understanding each factor is examined. The chapter lays the basis of the approach in the rest of the book. Pupils should always be conscious of how the contents relate to themselves, as consumer, and to the problems and techniques of producers with whom they may wish to pursue careers.

Time allocation
Section 1.1: 80 minutes; 1.2, 1.3, and 1.4: 80 minutes.

Extension work in this chapter
Section 1.1: exercise in data representation.

Worksheet and Assessment card Masters
FM1   Presenting data
FM19   Assessment card

1.1
HOW DO YOU CHOOSE?

Main ideas in this section

The pupils choose clothes for different reasons which can be analysed.

The reasons can be classified into aesthetic factors, performance factors, and price factors.

Assessing
(relevant
factors)

The first paragraph establishes the pupil as a consumer. Its object is to establish at the outset that the subject relates to everyday life. This can be approached either by letting pupils read the text or by a statement such as 'I expect you have all been shopping for clothes' from the teacher. An informal approach can help to establish this natural relationship with the world outside.

Few textile purchases are to satisfy a need: most are to satisfy a want. That want may be created by the display in the shop window or it may result from the purchaser's emotional desire just to buy something.

Figure 1.1
This picture helps to set the mood. It shows the pupil a typical place for garment purchase. It may be worth emphasizing that the recent purchase which will be analysed need not have been bought from that type of shop or from a shop at all (remember mail order, etc.).

Q 1

Communicating (writing)

Deciding criteria

This question is designed to make pupils think deeply about the reasons behind their choice. Encourage as many reasons as possible for the purchase, even if this requires considerable prompting. Most pupils will forget that quite trivial reasons (like the button style or decorative stitching) may be crucial.

There are two points to watch for in relation to the reasons given. Firstly, ensure that the pupils are not confused between discussing why they bought that type of garment and discussing why they bought that *particular* garment at that time. Secondly, it must be assumed that the garment fits correctly.

Figure 1.2
This cartoon shows fashionable clothing in different periods.

UNDERSTANDING THE CHOICE

Classifying

The division of reasons for purchase into aesthetic and social, performance, and price factors has two main purposes: it enables the contribution of science and technology to consumer judgments to be defined; and, in a wider context, it provides a way in which the pupils as consumers can approach purchasing in a scientific manner.

The method of approach above suggests, or apparently suggests, that the reasons for purchase are many, varied, and unconnected. The aim is to show that this is not so, and this section begins the process. Aesthetic factors are those which are subjective. They are matters of taste, individual judgment, and personal choice which other people may or may not agree with. For this reason they are peculiar to the individual pupil and no attempt should be made to impose on them judgments based on morality or taste. This is important. There should be no indication here, or at any stage, that the course is designed to limit or direct their choice in any particular direction.

Applying knowledge

The course provides the knowledge with which to make an informed choice; but in matters of aesthetics the decision will be entirely personal. Similarly, social factors are those reasons

2

where the choice made is influenced by peer group, religion, or custom. However, there is no question of right or wrong.

Performance factors are those factors which can be measured. They relate to technical standards which imply a value judgment which can be quantified, that is, measured. Price factors are likely to be the easiest to list. They are quite simply how much?

Q 2
The ideas suggested at the beginning of the section are ordered as below.

Classifying

Table T1.1

Aesthetics	Performance	Price
Attractive colour	washable	cheap
Different	well made	in the sale
Something special	I thought it would last a long time	
Went with my hair		
Matched the wallpaper	keep me warm in winter	
Went with some clothes I already had		
Like all my friends were wearing		
Makes me look grown up		
My girlfriend liked it		

Q 3
Check that pupils have answered question 2 correctly, or that their answers have been corrected before proceeding with question 3. Concentration and the use of both questions at this point ensures that the distinction between these important factors is clear. When everyone has had a chance to complete the division of their list ask them to add up the number of factors in each column. Use the results of question 2 as a guide.

Classifying

WHICH IS THE MOST IMPORTANT FACTOR?

It is extremely unlikely that anyone will have chosen anything but aesthetics as the most important factor. If they have, it is because they have chosen a very utilitarian item (such as a baby's nappy) to analyse. If this occurs it can be made use of

Assessing (relevant factors)

in discussing the order of importance. Some prompting such as 'Now, you have all listed aesthetics as the most important factor, what about performance?' can usually elicit the reply from some pupils that they 'don't care' about performance. A few well-directed questions like 'but surely you don't want it to fall apart the first time you wear it?' will quickly show that everyone is concerned about performance even if they are prepared to accept a low standard. This should be emphasized to ensure that no pupil believes that performance factors do not really enter into choice. The final consumer choice is a matter of relativities and that is what the rest of the chapter will show.

ORDER OF IMPORTANCE

Organizing data

Communicating (speech)

This aims to reverse the idea that aesthetics are always more important than performance, which is the impression that most pupils will have. If a pupil has produced an order of importance that puts performance first, this can be used as the example. If not, suggest a garment (such as a young boy's school trousers) where aesthetic factors are of low importance. Any form of survival clothing can also be used as an example.

Q 4

Communicating (speech)

By this stage pupils should have grasped the idea of the three factors. An oral response is all that is required. For the schoolboy's trousers, accept, quite readily, the fact that performance or cost may be placed first but clearly no one, except the awkward, will put aesthetics anywhere but last. Then draw the important conclusion that the same person can have a different order of priorities for different garments.

Figure 1.4
This is a visual guide to the sort of treatment small boys can give to their clothes and the necessity therefore to be concerned about performance.

Q 5
This question aims to start the process of showing the pupils how to make judgments when placed in the situation of another person. Clearly they cannot be very wealthy and very poor and are probably neither.

Figure 1.5
This is a visual guide to identifying the types of consumer.

Communicating (speech)

Again an oral response is probably all that is required. The important facts are that the wealthy person might put aesthetics first, performance second, and price last. Their

Reasoning logically

choices are wider. The very poor person would put cost first and probably performance second with aesthetics last. The conclusion can be drawn that different people will have different requirements for the same garment. If this provokes

4

discussion use one or two other items, such as bed linen or underwear.

RATING THE FACTORS

Communicating (maths)
This is a logical step towards a more quantitative evaluation of the importance of the three factors. Already, expressions of the relative importance of the factors as opposed to a simple order of priority have emerged. A pupil is unlikely to have said that for a particular item one factor is all important and that the other two don't matter at all. Draw on this now to show that it is possible to be more exact about the relative importance of the factors by awarding points to each one. A good scale is 1 to 10; where 10 represents very important and 1 represents negligible importance.

Do a trial run with an example such as a handkerchief. Do not be concerned about 1 or 2 points either way. No factor need be rated 10, and they can all be rated about equal.

Q 6
This exercise uses a scale for different textile items. The table below shows the probable answers.

Table T1.2

Item	Aesthetics	Performance	Price
Nappies	4	10	7
Car seat cover	7	5	6
Skirt	8	5	7
Parachute	1	10	1
Socks	6	6	6
Umbrella	6	9	7
Dishcloth	3	8	8
Anorak	7	6	7

Interpreting data
Remember that different people will have different requirements for the same item. The less critical items (*e.g.* socks) may have a wide divergence of opinion but few are likely to disagree about the parachute.

Q 7
Communicating (graphs)
This is an exercise in statistical representation. Two other answers are possible, although a bar chart is probably the best.

Worksheet FM1 describes methods of data presentation. It aims to help pupils appreciate household spending on textile items.

HOW DO YOU DECIDE WHAT TO CHOOSE?

You will need for each pupil or pair of pupils
Pictures of various garments

Applying
knowledge
This activity is designed to ensure that all the lessons covering the factors and their rating have been thoroughly understood and can now be applied in as near a practical shopping situation as possible. Any pictures of garments can be used but (preferably) they should be photographs, as fashion drawings often exaggerate the line. They should be in colour, since this is an important aesthetic factor, and should include male and female garments. An outfit could comprise a jacket with blouse and skirt or shirt and trousers. However, encourage the addition of accessories such as shoes, ties, bags, etc. Alternatively, household linens can be shown together with the curtains and carpeting for a room.

Q 8
Analysing
(data)
Pupils should rate the garments they have chosen exactly as they did in question 6. Collect together a number of results from individuals in the class and emphasize again the fact that different people have different requirements for the same item. Also show that for everyday items price is seldom the most important factor although it rates highly.

Refer back to question 6 for items where a matter of life and death is involved — price and aesthetics become of minor importance when considering a parachute. This can be illustrated by discussing anoraks and comparing one for everyday wear with one for use on an Antarctic expedition. Here, even colour is not an aesthetic factor. It becomes a performance factor as the colour orange is highly visible against a white background. As a final point, stress again that choice and the way the factors are rated is entirely personal. Clothes are a reflection of individual personality and the choice may not be appreciated by everyone. They reflect, often more than anything else, how people see themselves and the image they wish to project to others. This idea can be extended by showing a variety of pictures of individuals and producing comments of a social and psychological nature.

1.2
CONSUMERS AND SUPPLIERS

Main idea in this section

The pupils' decisions as consumers affect suppliers.

Here, pupils are brought face to face with commercial reality, which is behind the choices they make. They should be made to see that their decision as a consumer, which is entirely their

own, is of vital importance to the supplier. If the supplier cannot anticipate their needs, *i.e.* the way they balance the three
factors, then the supplier will not be successful. A useful discussion can result from considering local and national retailers who
are successful or who have not been successful. The large chain
stores are good examples of the former. For the latter, the
national press from time to time carries statements regarding
large firms in difficulties. Alternatively, the frequent bank-
ruptcy rate of retailers can be relied upon to ensure that a local
example is available.

1.3
WHERE DOES SCIENCE COME IN?

Main idea in this section

The properties of textiles can be controlled and predicted
by scientific means.

The examination of a material by scientific methods can give a
measure of its performance and can enable the reasons for this
performance to be understood. For this reason, scientifically
derived information can be used to predict the performance of a
textile item under various conditions. It is possible to compare
Communicating the performance of different fabrics and make such judgments
as 'one fabric is better than another in a certain respect'. The
one thing that this scientifically derived information cannot
Deciding determine is whether even the best is good enough. It is there-
criteria fore necessary for us to define the standards we require. This
should be brought out in discussion. An important point for all
pupils to realize is that performance factors can be understood
and predicted by scientific means.

Figure 1.7
This shows a fabric being subjected to a flammability test.
This is an important performance factor when dealing with
materials for childrens' nightwear, etc.

SCIENCE AND TECHNOLOGY
The information achieved by scientific means allows a 'technology' or field of knowledge to be built up. This means that the
possibility of a particular performance standard can be predicted. This information also shows how to achieve and measure a
standard of performance.

Q 9
Communicating This is a form of recall question to ensure that pupils
(speech) understand what is a performance standard or factor, as
opposed to the other two factors. At this stage exhaustive
exactness is not required. Suggested answers are: washable,

cleanable, durable, colourfast to wearing and cleaning, good
shape retention, original shape restorable by ironing, seams
do not break down, and collar retains its stiffness.

SCIENCE AND AESTHETICS

Q 10
This is a further recall question to ensure that pupils are clear
about what is an aesthetic requirement or factor. Again,
exhaustive exactness is not required. Suggested answers are:
colour, style (various aspects), handle, drape, transparency,
surface effects such as lustre or dullness, and surface design.

Deciding
criteria

Aesthetic factors are a matter of personal taste and generally
cannot be quantified. We cannot measure the handle of a silk
blouse. It can only be said to be something that most people
like though some do not. Whether a particular colour is liked
or not is also totally subjective, but whether we can achieve
that colour on a particular fabric, and then whether it will be
fast to washing is a performance factor and depends on technology. Very often a blouse or shirt can only be made in a
desired colour if the customer is prepared to accept very restric-
ted washing conditions.

Q 11
Reasoning
logically

Applying
knowledge

This tests the pupils' understanding of the ideas in this section.
Lightweight, soft fabrics would not be suitable for trousers
as they would not be sufficiently durable. A woollen coat
which cannot be worn in the rain is unsuitable. Cotton
curtains in the kitchen near a gas cooker are impractical
due to the fire risk — despite the pretty print.

SCIENCE AND PRICE
The parallel between aesthetics and price is clear. Although
money available can be quantified and sometimes people just
do not have money to buy a particular item, expenditure on
clothing is usually a matter of personal choice in terms of allocation of available resources. However, cost is affected by technical factors. Improving performance standards generally costs
money. This leads to the idea that a compromise may have to
be reached, in the question of both aesthetics and performance
factors in relation to cost.

1.4
COMPROMISES

Main idea in this section

The selection of an item may involve a compromise
between the three factors.

8

Concepts and skills	Pupils may be able to:
1.1 *How do you choose?* Choice factors: aesthetics, performance, and price. *Science/maths* Properties of materials. Classifying, Deciding criteria, Communicating (speech and writing).	Recall the three factors which influence choice and relate them to their own purchases. Explain the relative importance of each factor in relation to a wide variety of purchases. Suggest additional influences such as changing social and cultural attitudes and values.
1.2 *Consumers and suppliers* Marketing, consumer choice. *Science/maths* Market research, statistics. Analysing data, Assessing (relevant factors), Reasoning logically, Communicating (writing and graphs)	Distinguish between the variety of retail outlets. Recognize the relationship between retailer and consumer. Suggest ways in which retailers might predict how people will rate the three factors for these items.
1.3 *Where does the science come in?* Performance requirements. *Science/maths* Technical considerations. Deciding criteria, Reasoning logically, Applying knowledge.	Recognize a relationship between science, technology, and purpose. Suggest the factors a manufacturer might consider (*e.g.* fibre/yarn type, dye fastness, methods of construction, finishes, labelling, packaging) in producing textile items.
1.4 *Compromises* Choice factors. *Science/maths* How properties affect function. Deciding criteria, Communicating (writing and speech), Evaluating.	Identify the critical choice factor for given items. Discuss compromises between aesthetic, performance, and price factors for each item. Suggest how other factors such as the low cost of mass production, the high cost of limited production, or fashion may restrict consumers' choice.

This chapter has shown that individuals' requirements vary in terms of the three factors. It is now essential to realize that this balance or rather the balance that is accepted may be a compromise forced on the consumer by technical factors. Examples are numerous and will appear throughout the book. To understand which compromises are necessary and what they mean in terms of the three factors requires a scientific approach to textiles and a knowledge of the technology which stems from that approach.

Ideas for homework

Pupils could answer questions 6 and 7 (rating the aesthetic, performance and price factors for the articles in *figure 1.6*, and recording their results on a bar chart).

The Background reading for this chapter considers the job of the buyer for a chain of clothes shops. This article emphasizes that clothes do not just arrive in shops; that a great deal of work goes into the choices made by people like Roger Weston; and that this represents real occupations. It is particularly relevant to section 1.2 and may also be useful throughout the rest of the book.

CHAPTER 2

The clothes line

This chapter consists mainly of a series of investigations. Although this allows the operation of practical skills, its purpose is essentially to enable pupils to see the logical sequence whereby garments are built up from raw materials.

The method of approach is to start with a garment and dissect it into its component parts. Each step is examined in detail so that by reversing the process the pupil can see how the garment was originally produced.

The stages in this line of clothing production are then directly related to the organization and structure of the industry itself.

The investigations lead to conclusions about the nature of textiles which will be used in the next chapter. Each property which emerges is related to the three fundamental factors — aesthetics, performance, and price. These are the factors which affect consumer choice and were established in Chapter 1.

Time allocation
Sections 2.1 and 2.2: 40 minutes; 2.3: 40 minutes; 2.4: 80 minutes; 2.5, 2.6, and 2.7: 80 minutes.

Extension work in this chapter
Section 2.2: estimating and costing the thread in a garment.
Section 2.3: tests on trimming.
Section 2.5: measuring fibre specimens.
Section 2.7: work on the types of retailing.

Worksheet and Assessment card Masters
FM2   Why do we have curtains and carpets?
FM20   Assessment card

2.1
THE VARIETY OF TEXTILES

Main idea in this section

Textiles are used in a wide variety of ways.

This book will be predominantly concerned with clothing. In the space available, it is quite impossible to examine in any depth the great variety of textile products. It is most important to establish, and for the pupils to visualize, that this variety exists.

Figure 2.1
This provides clues for the quick recognition of textiles in four areas of use.

Q 1
Some of the items which could be mentioned are: flags, clothing (including racing suits, reflective vests, and helmet linings), tyres, banners, sun shades, deck chairs, sails, upholstery, curtains, carpet, aircraft tyres, aircraft interior furnishings.

This is probably best dealt with by written answers, which can be drawn together in class discussion.

Communicating (speech)

Discussion can be extended to other areas, *e.g.* the great variety of industrial uses — tarpaulins, conveyor belts etc., and in houses, glass fibre insulation, damp-proof courses (might be bituminized felt), roofing felt (bituminized), and scrim over plaster board joints are examples. Many types of small items may emerge: the front of 'hi-fi' loudspeakers; a painting on canvas; a fabric dust bag on a vacuum cleaner; and a more old-fashioned use is the mantle on gas lights. This last example has a modern equivalent in the fabric mantles used on camping gas lamps. By now, the idea that a wide variety of textiles results in a large industry should be understood.

Communicating (speech)

The pupils' text states here the course's intention of concentrating on garments and household textiles. The subsequent text will consider the properties required of fabrics. At this stage, the class may be asked to list some properties they expect to be important. Inevitably, they should mention strength or durability. As an example, they can be made to realize that just as durability is important for clothes, so it will be important in a carpet, a sack, and a fire hose. Therefore, conclusions drawn about fibre performance in relation to clothing durability can be applied to carpets and other textiles.

Q 2
Communicating (writing)

This question should be answered initially in written form followed by a class discussion. Depending on the composition of the class, the list may extend to particular religious or national garments, *e.g.* the sari. If not, they should be mentioned.

Figure 2.2
This shows forms of dress which not only relate to social custom but also to climatic conditions. The African tribesman wears little clothing as this is socially acceptable in a hot climate. The Arab wears enveloping garments to shield him from the sun, but also wears these garments as social custom outside his own country. Contrast Western dress (which in a fairly equable climate allows concentration on social

Assessing (relevant factors)

convention) with the dress of an Eskimo where the overriding factor is survival in adverse climatic conditions.

Extension work

Communicating (speech) If the class shows an interest in these ideas then time can be taken to discuss other nationalities and their dress and social customs. Explain that this type of study when undertaken to a fairly high level is called social anthropology. The restriction of subsequent discussion to conventional Western society dress is necessary. This should not be seen as denying the validity of national costume but rather as a reinforcement of the concept of the book as being relevant to what most pupils buy in their everyday shopping.

Worksheet FM2 applies some of these principles to textiles in the home.

2.2
BREAKING DOWN A GARMENT: STAGE ONE

Main idea in this section

A garment consists of a main body fabric and trimmings.

You will need for each group of pupils
Selection of old garments

Observing For this activity you should obtain old garments either from your own sources, from the pupils themselves, or from local Oxfam shops, jumble sales, etc.

It is important, for health reasons, that the garments should be cleaned before being used. This is for discussion by you as a first stage in preparation for later investigations. If ⚠ possible dissect a jacket or coat so that all the major components are found. Some other suitable garments for dissection are trousers, or blouses. The following are not suitable for this investigation.

Knitwear — since the main body fabric is difficult to dissect out in its entirety.
Garments where the main fabric is made from a filament yarn (*e.g.* a polyester jersey). The concept of yarn constructed from fibre is more difficult to understand using a filament yarn.
Fur or leather garments.

The dissection at this stage is mainly unpicking seams. There are a number of problems which are likely to be encountered.

There may be difficulty in preventing threads from breaking particularly on overlock seams. If necessary make an estimate of the length. Fusible interlinings will usually peel apart with

13

care and some effort, and anyway they do not cover the whole garment. Foam-backed fabrics should be left as they are. It can be explained that the foam is added as part of the processing of the fabric.

Q 3
This is simply a means of assessing whether the pupils are familiar with the large variety of trimmings present in garments. If the class as a whole has experience in dress or garment making the uses of various trimmings can be discussed. This helps to link the approach in this book to previous work on the subject. Refer to *figure 2.3* if necessary.

Extension work

Higher ability pupils can estimate the amount of thread in the garment. When the amount of thread in the garment has been estimated the following costing exercise could be undertaken. If thread costs 20p per 100 metres (industrial price), what is the thread cost as a percentage of the total garment cost? To obtain factory cost of the garment (approximately) divide the retail cost by 2.

Table T2.1
Thread consumption of various garments.

Garment	Metres of thread	Garment	Metres of thread
Women			
Apron	9	Skirt	92
Bathrobe	92	Slacks	117
Blouse	97	Slips	128
Coat	348	Vest	41
Dress	137	Waistcoat	55
Housecoat	239		
Nightie	69	*Men*	
Overall	220	Pants	73
Pants	82	Pyjamas	96
Pyjamas	87	Shirt	101
Raincoat	234	Vest	37

Figure 2.3
This shows a typical breakdown of a jacket into its component parts with the main fabric separated from all the trimmings.

2.3
LOOKING AT SOME OF THE PARTS

Main ideas in this section

Textiles have a unique combination of properties.

Aesthetic properties can be appreciated by visual and tactile means, but they are impossible to quantify.

This is a difficult section and the pupils will need careful guidance. Everyone is familiar with textiles and clothing as part of their everyday life. Very few will have thought to ask the question 'why textiles?' or 'why are my clothes built up this way?' This is a very important question. The whole of the textile industry exists on the basis that the production of fabric from fibre via yarn and its manufacture into garments is a pre-condition of the requirements for human apparel. In this section the characteristic properties which distinguish textiles from other possible materials for garments are established. In the next chapter it will be shown why textiles alone satisfy these requirements. The particular attribute of textiles is that they satisfy certain aesthetic requirements. These are the most difficult to designate, describe, and quantify.

HANDLING TESTS

You will need for each pair or group of pupils
Main body fabric

Pupils should select one of the main fabric pieces and feel it in the way shown in *figure 2.4*. Demonstrate the movements, then pose question 4.

Q 4

Observing

Assessing
(relevant
factors)

Communicating
(writing)

So that this question does not lead to confusion, give clear directions about what is meant by feeling the fabric as shown in *figure 2.4*. The property which is being shown is that of handle (*i.e.* surface feel). Some pupils may get some indication of the shape characteristic. This is most important and is explained in question 5. Suitable words to describe the handle of the fabric are smooth, knobbly, even, bobbly, soft, harsh, rough, scratchy, coarse, or silky.

Q 5

Observing

Assessing
(relevant
factors)

Textiles have drape and the ability to fall loosely and shape to the human figure. Easy distortion is allowed when required but textiles will return to their original shape when the source of that distortion is removed. This distortion may result from movements of the body itself (for example bending the arm) or from contact with outside objects (the seat of a chair). This

Communicating (writing)	means that a textile can move to accommodate much of the movement of the human body, and that it is comfortable to wear.
Practical skills	Suitable words to describe the drape of a fabric are floppy, pliable, hangs easily, moulds to the human shape, clingy, stiff.
Applying knowledge	Reinforce the idea that it is difficult to find the exact words to describe an aesthetic factor and hence quantify it. Contrast the idea of comfort and ease of movement when wearing a textile garment with wearing a suit of armour. *Figures 2.5* and *2.6* provide some clues.
Assessing (relevant factors)	Remind pupils about the three basic factors as detailed in Chapter 1. The important idea here is that the aesthetic factors we require and associate with textiles (as Chapter 3 will show) can only really be obtained by textile methods. They can be appreciated by visual and tactile means, whereas performance and price cannot.

It is true that an experienced buyer or textile technologist could infer from examination of a textile's aesthetic characteristics what fibres were present, how it was made, and hence how it would perform and how much it would cost in the current market. However, such a person could not be certain and would require scientific testing of performance and a definite price quotation to be sure.

Extension work
The same tests can be carried out on the trimmings, in particular the lining and interlining. The interlining may not have the same drape characteristics, but it can be pointed out that this is because its function is to give stiffness in certain parts of the garment.

2.4
BREAKING DOWN A GARMENT: STAGE TWO

Main ideas in this section

The construction of a fabric can be determined by dissection.

In fabric, yarns are interlaced.

You will need for each pair or group of pupils
Main body fabric

Hand lens
Variety of implements for dissecting, *e.g.* dissecting needle, sewing needle, scissors

Before the pupils start, remind them that they are only breaking down the garment one stage further. In this first stage, aim to get each group simply to separate yarns and get a pile of yarns alongside their fabric sample. *Figure 2.7* illustrates this.

Practical
skills

Selecting
equipment

Identifying
causes

Observing
Ask pupils to select from a variety of instruments which they think will be of most help in the dissection. The selection could be from a needle, a sewing needle, and a pair of scissors. Emphasize the use of the hand lens of low magnification as this heightens the idea of the breakdown into smaller and smaller components. The first breakdown was completed without optical aid. Although it seems obvious that if you pick up a pile of yarns they will fall apart, to emphasize the point make sure it *is* done. After pupils have picked up the pile of yarns, encourage a more detailed look at the way the yarns are interlaced, with the use of the hand lens.

Q 6
Communicating
(diagrams)
The diagrammatic representation of the interlacing of the yarns is a good exercise in reproducing visual observation.

At this stage, more able pupils may repeat the experiments with linings and interlinings (unless the interlining is of the non-woven variety).

2.5
BREAKING DOWN A GARMENT: STAGE THREE

Main ideas in this section

Yarns are made up of fibres.

A fibre consists of many millions of molecules.

You will need for each pair or group of pupils
Yarns taken from main body of fabric

Variety of implements for dissecting, *e.g.* dissecting needle, sewing needle, scissors
Powerful hand lens

Practical
skills

Selecting
equipment

Observing
This is the next stage in the dissection. Emphasize the use of a more powerful hand lens to reinforce the more and more detailed perspective the dissection is giving. Most yarns in the garments suggested for dissection will be made from staple fibres, so rotating the yarn in the fingers will open it more easily. Once the twist is removed a number of individual fibres can be obtained. If the fabric is constructed from filament yarn it will, inevitably, be multi-filament and so separate into finer components. *Figure 2.8* shows the dissection.

Extension work
Measuring

Communicating
(diagrams)
If good fibre specimens are obtained from staple fibre yarns, these can be measured and more able pupils may even draw a diagram or graph showing the distribution of lengths (as figure T2.1).

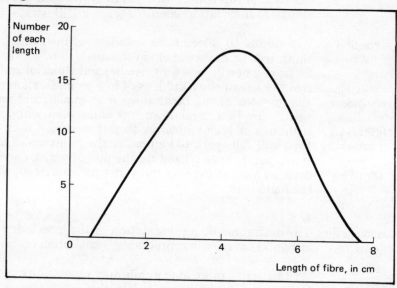

Figure T2.1

When the fibres have been separated it is important that the final stage of observation, under a microscope, takes place. Use of the microscope continues the emphasis on increasing detail.

EXAMINING THE FIBRES

You will need for each pair or group of pupils
Fibres taken from sample yarn

Powerful hand lens
Fine dissecting needle
Microscope

Observing

Reasoning
logically

The main purpose of allowing individual fibres to be seen more clearly under the microscope is to highlight the fact that this is the end of the line, or rather, the limit of visual observation. Nevertheless, pupils should realize that the fibres are built up of millions of tiny units (molecules) in exactly the same way as all other substances.

Link with school science
The molecule of any one fibre type is unique to it. This reinforces the link with the pure sciences, that the textile fibres are indeed chemical compounds.

Figure 2.9
This shows that there are techniques for examining the structure of fibre molecules. X-ray diffraction measures the scattering of X-rays by the atoms in the molecule and this is recorded on a photographic plate.

18

2.6
STAGE REVIEW

Main idea in this section

The chain built up so far can be reversed to give an idea of how a garment is assembled.

Q 7

Assessing
(relevant
factors)
This begins the process of structuring the concepts illustrated by the investigations into a rational sequence. Ensure that every pupil attempts to draw a correct chain.

Figure T2.2

Communicating
(diagrams)

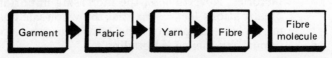

Observation
v
inference
Pupils must fully understand this concept before proceeding to the idea of reversing the chain. This could be introduced with the question 'what would reversing the chain represent?' The answers should ensure that the pupils understand that this is what happens in practice. (The chain is more representative of what is termed the 'cut and sew' garment business and is less appropriate to the fully fashioned knitwear trade.)

2.7
THE CHAIN OF TRADE

Main idea in this section

Each stage in the chain of trade represents a trade or industry.

Reasoning
logically
After the pupils have got the 'clothes line' chain right, ask the question 'what does it mean in practice?', looking for an answer which relates the chain to trade or industry. Pupils with some knowledge of textiles may object that the dyeing and printing processes are omitted as part of the textile chain. This can be explained in these terms: finishing and dyeing processes alter characteristics of fabrics but they do not change the basic stages of building up. In any event, as will be seen in later chapters, dyeing can take place at any stage of textile production.

A word of explanation may also be needed about the term 'the rag trade'. It was traditionally reserved for the women's dress, suit, and coat industry. In recent years the term has tended to become synonymous with the trade as a whole.

Figure 2.10

This shows the chain so far. This leads to question 8 where the final stages of retailer and consumer are to be added.

Communicating
(diagrams)
It would be advantageous for the pupils to draw the chain as depicted in *figure 2.10* and add the paths which complete the chain to the consumer. It is recommended that a complete sheet of paper is used for this as further additions are to be made in question 10.

Traditional terminology may cause confusion for some pupils. To be strictly accurate, the picture should include a reference to the distributive trades. This would account for those garments which go to wholesalers who buy clothes in bulk from factories and then sell them to small shops or retailers who are too small to undertake their own direct contact with the factories. Nevertheless, the increasing importance of large retail organizations has meant that the wholesale business is now very much less important. The best term which will relate to the pupils' experience is 'retailing'.

Q 9
It is important that pupils realize that retailing is not simply confined to shops. Even within the group 'shops' there are department stores, variety chain stores, and small or large independent stores. In addition, there is a whole range of methods of retailing — mail order catalogues, direct mail order, party plan, and market stalls.

Extension work
If the forms of retailing produce interest, pupils should be encouraged to make lists of various types in their own locality and nationwide. This again heightens the feeling of relevance.

Finally, although the book is primarily concerned with garments, remind pupils that there are other textile items and these too are part of the chain. This is illustrated in *figure 2.14*.

Q 10
Applying
knowledge
Piece goods are fabrics bought for use in home garment and household textile making. That means that they jump part of the chain. The chain for piece goods and that for carpets is shown on the next page.

Household textiles generally follow the same pathway in the chain up to the fabric stage. They usually require much less making-up than clothing (*e.g.* sheets), although in recent years, with the advent of continental quilts and fitted sheets, more making-up is required. For household textiles, the fabric producing firms may do their own making-up, but this is nonetheless another step in the chain. It can be written simply as making-up since it is certainly not part of the clothing trade. The item then passes to the retailer. It is useful here to remind

Figure T2.3

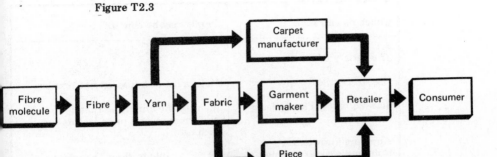

pupils that the three factors — aesthetics, performance, and price — apply equally to household textiles. Whereas fashion or aesthetics played a fairly limited role fifty years ago in the bed linen market, fashion now plays a very large part.

Figure 2.13
This photograph illustrates the changing fashions in bed linen.

Assessing
(relevant
factors)

As a final point in the chapter, remind pupils of one other important aspect of the chains. While each chain represents successive steps in building up a finished textile item and passing it on to the consumer, it also shows that at each stage of the chain people are making decisions about what they are producing and whether it will satisfy the ultimate consumer. That is, they are all attempting to attain the right balance of factors — aesthetics, performance, and price.

Idea for homework
The Background reading in this chapter illustrates the continuing international significance of cotton, the World's most important textile fibre. The subject has many aspects to it (historical, social, technical) which can be developed in homework.

Concepts and skills	Pupils may be able to:
2.1 *The variety of textiles* Uses of textiles. *Science/maths* Properties of materials. Applying knowledge, Communicating (writing), Assessing (relevant factors).	Make a list of house uses of textiles. Identify the critical aesthetic, performance, and price factors for each use. Devise a table to show the relative importance of the three factors for a variety of garments.
2.2 *Breaking down a garment: stage one* Garment construction. *Science/maths* Structure related to function. Costing. Observing, Applying knowledge, Communicating (diagrams), Estimating.	Draw an outline of the component parts of a garment and identify them. Identify the fibres used and suggest alternatives. Estimate the likely quantities of fabric and trimmings.
2.3 *Looking at some of the parts* Properties of textiles related to wear and comfort. *Science/maths* Properties of textiles related to fibre and fabric structure. Observing, Applying knowledge, Communicating (writing and diagrams), Practical skills, Assessing (relevant factors).	Suggest some of the properties of textiles related to wear and comfort. Relate these properties to the body's movements, such as bending and stretching. Relate the properties to the effects of wear and maintenance, and function. Say that interlinings, linings, and other trimmings can be used to reduce distortion in wear. Say where each may be used in garments.
2.4 *Breaking down a garment: stage two* Structure of textiles. *Science/maths* Use of magnifying instruments; magnification. Observing, Communicating (writing and diagrams), Identifying causes, Practical skills.	Dissect and identify correctly the component parts of a garment. Distinguish between different weave patterns. Record in writing or diagrammatically the differences in various weave patterns.

Concepts and skills	Pupils may be able to:
2.5 *Breaking down a garment: stage three* Yarn structure. *Science/maths* Properties of materials. Measurement. Magnification. Observing, Communicating (writing and diagrams), Practical skills.	Distinguish between different arrangements of fibres in a yarn. Using a microscope, look at and draw a variety of other fibres.
2.6 *Stage review* and **2.7** *The chain of trade* Stages of manufacture, supply, and distribution. *Science/maths* Textile technology. Flow diagrams. Applying knowledge, Communicating (writing and diagrams), Assessing (relevant factors).	Draw a flow chart to explain the chain of production of a garment. Name the process of manufacture at each stage in the chain. Reverse the chain and explain what this means. Suggest some advantages and disadvantages to the consumer of the different forms of retail outlet, *e.g.* shops, superstores, markets, postal buying.

CHAPTER 3

Why textiles – why not plastics?

Chapter 2 identified the characteristics of textiles including those desirable aesthetically. This chapter considers whether these characteristics might not be more easily obtained from other materials. Textile production is shown to be relatively expensive, and alternative, cheaper possibilities are examined. The oldest known form of clothing based on animal skins is considered and shown to be an expensive process, as well as being rather impractical. Paper and plastics are examined but, although relatively cheaper, are shown to have aesthetic and performance defects compared with textiles. The reason for the superiority of textiles lies in the fibre itself and the retention of its desirable properties in subsequent manufacture.

Time allocation
Section 3.1 and 3.2 together: 40 minutes; 3.3 and 3.4 together: 160 minutes; 3.5: 40 minutes.

Extension work in this chapter
Section 3.2: discussion of life-style of prehistoric man; estimation of the number of skins needed to make a garment.
Section 3.3: making up garment sections.
Section 3.4: cost comparisons.

Worksheet and Assessment card Masters
FM8   Fabric strength
FM21   Assessment card

3.1
WHY SO MANY PROCESSES?

Main ideas in this section

Textile fabric production involves a large number of processes.

The greater the number of processes, the greater the cost.

Deciding criteria

The first part of this section is a revision of Chapter 2. It links up the concept of the clothes line or chain of production for the next stage of development. The stages shown are fibre to yarn and yarn to fabric. Even then the fabric is not complete; it has to be 'finished'. This means that it has to undergo a few more processes before it is ready to go to the garment manufacturer. At this stage any question relating to non-woven fabrics can be avoided by saying that they represent only a small percentage of textile production for clothes and that they will

24

be dealt with in Chapter 7. Do not spend much time on the 'finishing' processes at this stage. These will be explained in Chapter 12.

Q 1

Q 1

Communicating
(diagrams)

Communicating
(diagrams)

This ensures that the large number of processes involved is understood. There are three different processing steps: fibre to yarn, yarn to fabric, and fabric to finished fabric.

Q 2

Here the answer is three. Even this is a simplification as, for example, finishing itself is a number of small steps.

The idea is now developed by concentrating on price or cost. Each processing step must cost money: the more processing steps the greater the cost. To start with, each step must require different machinery, and machinery is expensive.

Q 3 and figure 3.2

Suggesting
hypotheses

Assessing
(relevant
factors)

Reasoning
logically

The question relates to economics and financial costing but its value is that it shows once again the inter-relationship between textile science and other disciplines. *Figure 3.2* is an aid to the answer. Each processing step will probably require a different factory or different part of a large factory. This must stand on extra land, pay extra rates, use extra services (water, electricity, etc.), and employ more workers. The goods may have to be transported from one processing step to another. All these things cost money. The question which should arise is 'If textiles require so many processes, which cost money, why can't it be done more cheaply?' Emphasize again that what is being looked for is a two-dimensional material which will cover a human body.

3.2
SKINS AND FURS

Main ideas in this section

Skins and furs have been used for clothing from prehistoric times.

These are not cheaper than textiles and they are sometimes impractical.

Applying
knowledge

Lead on from the idea of searching for an alternative two-dimensional material. You could ask 'What two-dimensional material has been used for clothing since prehistoric times?' If necessary prompt with the words 'cave man'.

Extension work

You could have a detailed discussion of the life and times of 'cave men': their social customs, way of life, and so on. Pupils could do some research.

The preparation of material for clothing from animal skins involves several processes (point out the parallel with finished fabrics). These processes may be expensive, not least because they are time-consuming. Processing in factories is obviously quicker, but it still takes a relatively long time to cure and tan skins.

Having shown that skins and furs need several processes now consider some more possible price disadvantages. The first of these is the cost of the raw material: the skin or hide itself. Concentrate first on wild animals and on those which have traditionally been hunted for clothing (in particular the cat family, such as the leopard or ocelot in *figure 3.5*). Point out that these species have become endangered as a result of hunting. Parallel with it the use of animal skins such as crocodile, for other items. Ostriches were almost destroyed by the demand for feathers for hats. Apart from moral considerations, the result of this is to make the raw material difficult to obtain and therefore expensive. Turning now to farm animals, there is clearly less difficulty in supply. However, even a sheep is not produced and grown to maturity overnight, and the provision of land and feedstuffs over this period of time costs money.

In comparing fur and (in particular) sheepskin coats with those made from woollen textiles there will always be examples of high-fashion woollen textile coats that are more expensive than sheepskin. The comparison should clearly be based on bulk production woollen textile coats compared with sheepskin coats. Within the cost of the woollen textile coat is the cost of the lining and interlining (see Chapter 2). These are not present, or only occasionally present, in sheepskin coats. The economics here are clear. The sheep can be sheared once a year for a number of years (*figure 3.6*) whereas it can only give one sheep-

skin. If a pupil mentions the money realized from the meat point out that a sheep sheared eventually gives as much meat as a sheep killed for its skin.

The size of the skin is important, and of course not all the skin is usable. It may be thin around the leg areas of the animal or it may be damaged.

Extension work

Pupils could estimate the number of skins of different animals needed to make a three-quarter length coat. A cow, sheep, leopard, and mink can be used as examples. There is a mathematical exercise here if required. For this purpose, assume that the skin area of an animal is approximately the square of its length. Therefore, if a cow is 2 m long its skin area will be

2 m × 2 m, that is 4 m². A mink approximately 0.3 m long has a skin area of 0.09 m². So for a given size of coat you will

Analysing (data)

need 4 ÷ 0.09 = 44.4 times as many minks as cows. Pupils could work out similar ratios on the basis that a leopard is 1.5 m and a sheep 1 m long. In reality, many skins are narrower than their length.

Link with school maths
By the age of fourteen most pupils will have covered work on simple proportion.

Q 4
If on average one cow yields one three-quarter length coat then clearly about 45 minks are needed.

Figure 3.8
This shows how all the skins are utilized to make a mink coat, clearly illustrating the cost involved in processing.

Identifying causes

So far the limitations of skins and furs have been discussed with regard to price factors, but there is also the important factor of comfort. There is no need to go into the reasons for this. It will be quite clear from the pupils' own experience. They are not suitable for warm climates.

Q 5
This question reminds pupils that different people can have

Communicating (speech)

different requirements in terms of aesthetics, performance, and price. An Eskimo faced with intense cold will find the performance advantage of furs so necessary that even the

Applying knowledge

problems of obtaining animal skins will be overcome. However, the limited number of Eskimos means that the demand on the animal supply for fur will also be limited. And the fur coat will last a long time as skins and furs are very durable. The durability of furs is not so important in more temperate climates because of the aesthetic and social demands of changing fashion.

3.3
PAPER AND PLASTICS

Main ideas in this section

Paper and plastics are cheap two-dimensional materials.

They are not aesthetically suitable for clothing.

Approach this section with the clear intention of finding a cheaper alternative to textiles. This could be done by posing

Applying knowledge

the question 'If skins and furs are at least as expensive as textile fabrics because they involve several processes, can you think

of any material which has fewer production processes?'
A prompt here is 'When you go to a shop, what do they usually
give you free?' The answer is the wrapping material and the
reason is that it is cheap. Make sure that pupils realize that what
is being looked for is a wrapping material for the human body.
Why not use the two wrapping materials commonly used in
shops — paper and plastics?

Communicating
(speech)

It is not necessary to go into great detail about paper and plastic
production, though these are illustrated in *figures 3.9* and *3.10*.
The important point is that they involve fewer processes from
raw material to final product. Plastic chips are the raw material
of plastic sheets. One can say that the plastic chips are equivalent
to fibres in textile processing though even here fibres present, in
the case of synthetics, a stage in processing beyond fibre chips.
Paper starts with wood pulp and again the process is relatively
simple.

Reasoning
logically

Q 6

This question can be answered verbally, to ensure that the
pupils understand the reasoning above. To be strictly accurate,
the answer depends on the cost of the raw material. But if the
plastic and fibre raw material were the same price then plastic
sheet would be much cheaper than fibre. If pupils query this
then quote examples where the same raw material is converted
into plastics and fabrics. One such example is polyester which,
as a plastic, is made into a sheet and is then cut up and used as
the backing for recording tape.

Communicating
(speech)

Suggesting
hypotheses

Q 7

This is a final question to show how cheap clothing made from
paper could be. The question asks for an estimate of how
many jackets could be made from a Sunday newspaper. An
average paper has 40 pages or 10 double sheets. At 2½ sheets
per garment, 4 garments could be made from a 40p newspaper.
That is 10p per garment for material (and that includes the cost
of printing!). So pose the question 'Why don't we use paper and
plastics?' and then return to the three factors: aesthetics, performance, and price.

Communicating
(maths and
speech)

MAKING GARMENTS FROM DIFFERENT MATERIALS

You will need for each pair or group of pupils
Paper, plastic sheet, and fabric pieces of the same weight, cut out in
various pattern shapes ready for assembly by the pupils
Thread

Scissors
Pins
Sewing machine

Warning: plastic sheeting can cause suffocation if not
ventilated properly.

The purpose of this work is not to develop practical skill in making garments, although this is a useful by-product. The main purpose is to find out whether paper and plastics are aesthetically suitable for clothing. For this reason the pattern pieces are best cut out before the lesson so time is not wasted at this stage.

The paper, plastic, and fabric should be of as near the same thickness as possible. Use strong wrapping paper. Newspaper, although cheap, is far too easily split. Polythene or polypropylene makes a suitable plastic sheet and is commonly available from hardware stores or builders' merchants. A woven cotton shirting fabric will suffice for the textile fabric. The best garments to make are simple knee-length skirts (without waistband and zip). At least one group should make an important garment section such as a sleeve. *Figure 3.11* shows a model wearing examples of clothing made from textile fabric, paper, and plastic.

Extension work

Other garments and sections of garments can be made. Examples are simple trousers or tunic tops.

When the garments or sections have been made, the handling tests in Chapter 2 should be carried out. The garments should then be worn and observed in simple activities: sitting and then standing up, bending the arms, bending the knees. The lack of drape and the poor recovery from simple distortions of the paper and plastic garments will be all too apparent.

3.4
LOOKING AT THE PROBLEMS

Main ideas in this section

Clothes made of paper and plastics have poor aesthetic properties compared with textiles.

Textiles are generally more durable (a performance factor) than paper or plastics.

First it is necessary to highlight the difference in the aesthetic properties of paper and plastics on the one hand and textiles on the other. These should have become apparent in the previous section. Again remind pupils of the three factors (aesthetics, performance, and price). Paper and plastics are superior to textile fabrics on price, but poorer on aesthetics. Now what about performance? Only one property is considered, but it is the fundamental one of strength.

TEAR STRENGTHS OF MATERIALS

You will need for each pair of pupils
Piece of plastic, 10 cm × 10 cm
Piece of paper, 10 cm × 10 cm
Piece of fabric, 10 cm × 10 cm
Spring balance

Suggesting hypotheses

Designing tests

As part of the investigation ask pupils to devise their own strength test using the three materials — plastic, paper, and textile fabric. Their methods are likely to be effective in showing the differences, but not very reproducible. Show them the method illustrated in figure T3.1. Using weights as an alternative to the spring balance is illustrated in *figure 12.5*.

Figure T3.1

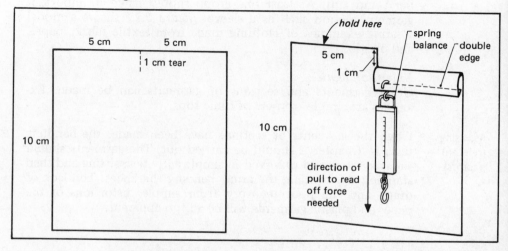

Observing

By putting a small tear or cut in the fabric, one of the obvious weaknesses of paper and plastics becomes apparent. As a textile fabric tears it breaks one yarn after another, but there is always a new yarn to be broken. There is no such resistance in paper or plastics.

Identifying causes

Observing

On the subject of plastic garments, a pupil may mention the plastic mac. This is a very good illustration of how plastics are inferior to textile fabrics for this type of light clothing. The original plastic macs were made simply from vinyl plastic sheet. They very quickly tore at any part where strain was applied, such as buttons and buttonholes, pockets, and across the shoulders. Plastic macs stuck up with Sellotape were a common sight. Sales dropped dramatically, and the plastic mac is now almost always made from a plastic-coated nylon fabric.

Reasoning logically

Paper pants may also be mentioned. Although these were fashionable in the late 1960s, they now constitute only a very small part of the market. The paper material used is not strong enough to withstand washing and only just about able (usually) to stand a day's wear. This use of paper depends on the fact that it is such a simple garment and can be made cheaply enough for some people to consider throwing it away. Even so, consumers pay heavily for the advantages.

Extension work

Communicating
(maths and
writing)
Ask pupils to compare the cost of a pair of cotton pants which might last 50 weeks with the cost of 50 pairs of paper pants. Current prices should be obtained from local retailers.

3.5
WHY ARE TEXTILES BETTER?

Main ideas in this section

Textiles have been shown to be superior to paper and plastics on aesthetic and performance factors.

The results of the experiments link these desirable properties to the fibre itself.

List the three factors (aesthetics, performance, and price) and emphasize again the superiority (generally) of textile fabrics. Even with their poorer aesthetic properties, paper and plastics might have been thought to have held a good share of the market simply by price alone. A reminder of the findings of Chapter 1 will explain why this is not so. Aesthetics are so important in textiles for everyday clothing in Western society that a large price advantage is not sufficient to overcome it. The investigation in section 3.4 should help to explain why textile fabrics have this superiority. This allows pupils to understand the whole purpose of the chapter: that is, to answer the question 'Why does the textile industry exist?'.

If the textile fibres obtained in section 2.3 are not available, other fibres may be obtained from the cotton fabric used in the investigations in this chapter. It is difficult for pupils to obtain a handling sensation from a single fibre, though a small bunch of fibres will make this easier. They should, however, be able to see the way individual fibres will drape and move easily when distorted. The whole expertise and rationale of the textile processes then become clear. They have evolved over the centuries as a way of preserving the desirable characteristics present in the fibre which is built up into an individual yarn and then into two-dimensional fabric. At the same time, wherever possible, these properties are enhanced. A clear example is strength. Individual fibres and bundles of fibres have no great strength but, as Chapter 5 will show, the method of joining fibres together in yarns retains aesthetic properties while allowing strength to be built up. This strength is available in two-dimensional form when the fabric is produced.

Observing

Identifying
causes

Assessing
(relevant
factors)

Applying
knowledge

Concepts and skills	Pupils may be able to:
3.1 *Why so many processes?* and **3.2** *Skins and furs* Fabric production. Process/cost relationship. *Science/maths* Textile technology. Analysing data, Applying knowledge, Deciding criteria, Communicating (speech and writing), Suggesting hypotheses, Assessing (validity).	Name the animals used to make clothes. Discuss the advantages and disadvantages of each. Suggest factors which may affect their use, such as endangered species, cost of production, fashion trends. Discuss aesthetic, performance, and price factors for particular items (*e.g.* comfort, water repellence, ease of maintenance).
3.3 *Paper and plastics* Properties of materials. *Science/maths* Textile technology. Applying knowledge, Using references, Observing, Deciding criteria, Communicating (writing, diagrams, and speech), Practical skills.	Identify and list the properties of paper and plastics. Give examples of uses of paper and plastics which could replace textiles. Identify the raw materials and the stages of production of paper and plastics. Draw flow charts to illustrate these.
3.4 *Looking at the problems* and **3.5** *Why are textiles better?* Durability. Tear strengths. *Science/maths* Properties of materials. Applying knowledge, Deciding criteria, Communicating (speech and writing), Suggesting hypotheses, Designing tests, Assessing (accuracy).	State the performance properties required for specialist clothing, *e.g.* mechanic, chef, surgeon. Discuss aesthetic, performance, and price factors of paper and plastics for these uses. Identify performance required for a variety of uses and relate them to plastics, paper, and textiles. Suggests factors other than durability which are important, such as comfort in wear, frequency of use, cost, and hygiene.

Ideas for homework

Pupils could find out all the living creatures which are used to make clothing items. They could then be asked to identify which of them are endangered species.

Pupils could write an essay on the discovery and production of polythene. (This will require some reference material.)

They could make a collage of the uses of paper using photographs from newspapers and magazines.

The idea of materials and their appropriateness to a function is taken up in the Background reading. The article concerns a student of jewellery and her explorations of the uses of plastic and of the application of science and technology to art.

CHAPTER 4

Fibres: the first step in the line

The previous chapter showed that the fibre is the essential first step in textile production. It demonstrated that its properties are the reason for the success of textile fabrics in clothing compared with other possibilities. Before considering the detailed science and technology of fibres and fabrics, it is necessary to ask 'what fibres?'. The fairly limited number of fibres used commercially in clothing and household textiles is then related to aesthetics, performance, and price. The idea that the relative importance of the fibres used is simply another way of stating how successful each is in achieving a compromise between the three factors is introduced. The chapter also defines the difference between generic and trade names.

Time allocation
Section 4.1: 40 minutes; 4.2: 40 minutes; 4.3: 20 minutes; 4.4: 20 minutes.

Extension work in this chapter
Section 4.2: investigation of advertising of fibres.
Section 4.2: consideration of usage of wool in World terms and reasons for differences.
Section 4.4: use of news media to assist in the prediction of World price trends for fibres; assessment of fibres in terms of aesthetics, performance, and price.

Worksheet and Assessment card Masters
FM3   Looking at fibres with a microscope
FM4   How do fibres react to burning?
FM22 Assessment card

4.1
MANY ARE KNOWN — FEW ARE CHOSEN

Main ideas in this section

There are many fibres in existence but only a few are used for clothing.

A balance between price, performance, and aesthetics is necessary when choosing a fibre. The most popular fibres, on average, give the best combinations of these factors.

Fibres can be classified into a number of groups.

This section begins by asking the question 'what is a fibre?'. Most people have a very clear idea what a fibre is but have difficulty in putting it into words. Sooner or later the words 'fine' and 'hair-like' will come up but this is not an accurate, scientific way of describing a fibre. It simply relates a fibre to another recognizable shape. It would be almost as easy to say what a fibre is not. It is not like a lump of coal; it is not like a piece of glass. It is, of course, a solid, not a liquid, like water, or a gas. By using these, perhaps all too obvious examples, the way is prepared for a more scientific definition. A fibre is a material whose length is many times greater than its cross-sectional width. Its cross-sectional width is very small — certainly less than one millimetre and usually considerably finer.

Deciding
criteria

Figure 4.1
This shows some fibres in cross-section. Although the cross-sections of fibres are often represented as a circle, this is really only true for certain synthetic fibres — as will be seen in Chapter 6. Natural fibres have a variety of cross-sectional shapes. Man-made fibres can be made in different shapes. The text moves now to the concept that there are many fibres which are known but few which are chosen.

Q 1
This is simply a selection of fibres chosen at random and of no particular individual significance. A totally different list could have been chosen with equal effect. One or two names may be known to the pupils, *e.g.* modacrylic, vicuna, kapok. Pupils will query pineapple, but the fibre is, of course, obtained from the leaves of the plant.

Communicating
(writing)

Figure 4.2
This shows another aspect of natural fibres: the variety of sources. The camel gives camel hair fibres. This fibre is expensive but is nevertheless used in knitwear and in coats. The traditional camel coat is usually made from wool in a camel colour. The Angora rabbit gives Angora hair fibre which is often blended with wool in knitwear. Note that the fibre from the rabbit should not be confused with the fibre obtained from the Angoran goat. The goat is the source of mohair. The palm tree produces coconuts. The fibre from this has already been discussed. The silkworm produces a cocoon from which silk fibres can be unwound.

The conclusion is already obvious that although all fibres conform to the definition given at the beginning of the chapter, and have certain similarities in that they can be converted into textile fabrics, there are wide variations in their properties.

Sisal is obtained from the leaves of plants. It comes from a plant grown mainly in Mexico. It has a particularly harsh handle, and may be familiar due to its use in mats and rough twine. It is very resistant to rotting. Contrast this with alginate, a fibre produced from seaweed, which dissolves in water. Its use depends on this property. It is woven into fabrics with other fibres and when dissolved out in subsequent processing leaves a patterned effect. Its handle is, therefore, of little importance. Vicuna, on the other hand, has a high aesthetic value because of its handle. Sisal is cheap, vicuna expensive. Both, however, are used very little for clothing: sisal because its aesthetic value is very low and vicuna because its price is very high. Contrast this with fibres that everyone knows (like wool and cotton) and the need to balance all three factors will emerge.

Q 2

Communicating
(writing)

This asks the pupils to think of garments or textile items and a fibre particularly associated with them. As a start, natural fibres could be considered, such as cotton handkerchiefs, silk ties, woollen suits, woollen knitwear, cotton shirts.

Identifying
causes

Ask why there is a particular association. The reason is that for each item you need a particular combination of aesthetics, performance, and price. For example, a cotton handkerchief must be reasonably soft, easily washed, absorbent, and relatively cheap. A woollen jumper must be soft, bulky, reasonably hard-wearing, and (ideally) easily washable. Since wool is not easily washable in its pure form, why is wool used for jumpers rather than cotton which is cheaper and washable? The answer is that the aesthetics of wool are greatly preferred, and that it is easier to obtain a bulkier, and hence warmer, garment. (Note that in recent years cotton sweatshirts have become very popular, particularly as the price of wool has risen to a far greater extent than the price of cotton.)

Classifying

The classification of fibres is straightforward. The only area which sometimes causes confusion is the distinction within man-made fibres between the regenerated and the synthetic. Man-made fibres are those fibres which are not grown naturally in the form in which they are used. Thus, although viscose is obtained from a natural material (mainly wood pulp), it is made by regenerating the cellulose from wood pulp and dissolving it in various chemicals (see Chapter 6). The definition of man-made also includes synthetic fibres which are made of complex chemical compounds (as are the natural and regenerated fibres) but they are built up in chemical factories from simple chemicals.

Q 3

This question ensures that pupils understand the classification of fibres.

Figure T4.1

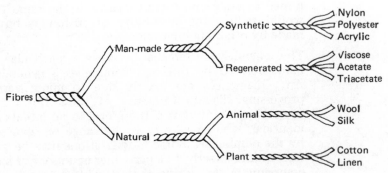

The specific fibres mentioned above comprise 99 per cent of the fibres used for clothing and household textiles in Western Europe.

Figure 4.3
This illustrates the sources of the main natural fibres.

4.2
GENERICS AND OTHERS

Main ideas in this section

Many fibres and fabrics are known by generic and brand names.

The use of brand names has certain advantages for the manufacturer.

Generic names and the percentage of fibres present can be found on clothing labels. Brand names are sometimes on these labels.

The distinction between the generic name and the brand name still causes confusion, even in textile textbooks. There is no problem with natural fibres, although individual companies have on occasions attempted to introduce brand names for yarns and fabrics which have a particular fibre composition. One of the best known of these is Viyella, which is a blend of wool and cotton fibres.

These distinctions began with man-made fibres when individual companies began producing a particular generic type and wished to safeguard their lead in the field by using a brand name which could not be copied by another firm as opposed to the generic name which could. Polyester is a good example. The fibre was first produced in the laboratories of Calico Printers Association in Lancashire, but the rights to manufacture the fibre and sell it Worldwide (except in the United States) were obtained by ICI. They gave the name Terylene to the polyester fibre they produced. Subsequently, other manufacturers produced

Classifying

Communicating
(speech)

37

polyester, but they could not call it Terylene. In this way, ICI hoped to build up a 'brand loyalty' to the name Terylene which would reduce the possibility of customers buying polyester made by other manufacturers.

The chemical difference between a particular generic fibre manufactured by different companies is generally very small. Any differences are mainly due to minor variations in the processing. The performance of these fibres from the consumer's point of view is therefore, to all intents and purposes, identical. What may vary is the range of fibre sizes produced by the companies. Some modifications may be made to fit the fibres more exactly to a particular end use. For instance, a fibre company might decide that it wished to sell its fibres in a particular textile area, such as curtaining and drapes. The company would work very closely with manufacturers of those particular fabrics to produce exactly the right construction of fabric and finish for that particular area of use. The company's particular branded fibre might be slightly better, though not necessarily so, than if the goods were made using another branded fibre of the same generic type. A typical example of this was the use made by ICI of their Terylene fibre to develop a textured yarn for the jersey fabric trade. This yarn was called Crimplene. As a result of the expertise built up by ICI with jersey manufacturers in the 1960s, Crimplene established a real lead in this area. For several years ICI held their lead, although other polyester fibre manufacturers have now moved in and use exactly the same processes to give exactly the same fabrics with their polyester yarns.

The two largest fibre manufacturers in the United Kingdom are ICI which makes polyester and nylon, and Courtaulds which makes polyester, acrylic viscose, acetate, and triacetate, as well as some other less important fibres.

WHY USE BRAND NAMES?

Q 4

Communicating (speech)

Applying knowledge This question, for which a verbal answer is sufficient, is designed to test whether pupils can link their own shopping experience with the discussion. Answers include Terylene, Crimplene (a form of Terylene), Dacron, Diolen, Fortrel, Trevira, Tergal, Terital, and Tetoron.

Note that there are companies which make polyester fibres, particularly in the Far East, which do not give their products a brand name.

ICI and Courtaulds also make fibres in other parts of the World. This can be through their own company or in a company they have set up jointly with a company in that other country. ICI, for example, has a joint company with American Celanese in the United States making a polyester fibre called Fortrel. Foreign companies make fibres in the United Kingdom. The American company, Monsanto, make acrylic fibre in Northern Ireland and the German company, Hoechst, make polyester fibre in the same area.

Q 5

Reasoning
logically

The reason is clearly economic. A factory producing fibre needs to be large to be economically viable. Remember, fibre is only the first stage in the line; it must be sold to the textile producer and transported there. It would clearly be cheaper for Monsanto to make their fibre in Northern Ireland and to sell it in the United Kingdom and other parts of Europe (provided they can build a factory big enough) rather than to ship the fibre all the way from the United States.

Q 6

The reason why many fibre manufacturers guard their brand names has already been discussed. *Figure 4.4* shows an old advertisement.

Extension work
Pupils could be asked to collect advertisements which contrast the advertising of fibres today with the one illustrated.

The trend today has been to move away from fibre brand names. A more widespread use of the generic name is becoming more common. There are a number of reasons for this. As more and more manufacturers all over the World began to produce man-made fibres, the number of brand names grew enormously and the public tended to become more and more confused. Fibre manufacturers selling into a market which had an already established brand name for say, a polyester fibre, did not want to go to the expense of advertising their particular polyester fibre and tended to rely on the generic name. Also, in the United Kingdom, large retail organizations and some textile manufacturers wanted to buy a particular type of fibre at the most competitive price and so did not want to be tied to a particular brand available from only one manufacturer. Finally, the E.E.C. regulations attempted to clear up the confusion by demanding that whether or not a brand name was used, the generic name should be visible on the item at the point of sale.

Q 7

Deciding
criteria

These regulations were an attempt to reduce confusion for the consumer. At the same time, since all fibres of a particular generic type are more or less the same, the customer would not get an inferior performance in one fabric compared with another with the same basic fibre content. Unfortunately, this

39

is only completely true if one compares fabrics of identical construction and finish. The use of the generic fibre name does not guarantee that the fabric has been produced in the best possible way. Because of the control and quality checking that many fibre manufacturers do, a fibre brand name may be a guarantee of correct fabric manufacture even though the fibre may not differ from the unbranded product. On the other hand it may not.

LOOKING AT LABELS

You will need for each pair of pupils
Selection of clothing and textile items (with labels)
Pen and paper

Observing

This is a simple exercise to find out what textiles are made from and to distinguish between generic and brand names. Try to obtain a variety of different garments as this will increase the variety of fibres. The regulations are strict on the correct

Communicating (writing) percentage of fibres being shown. However, if a large number of fibres are present, for example in fabrics made from re-claimed fibres, the regulations do permit the term 'other fibres' to be used.

Q 8

Assessing

The answer to this depends on the type of clothing which has been selected.

Extension work

Communicating (maths) A bar chart could be made showing the usage of the various fibres or fibre blends.

The standards of natural fibres vary due to growing conditions. As a result the variations within a particular natural fibre will be greater than variations in man-made fibres. Also, there are

Identifying causes no brand names for natural fibres which consumers can use. Differences can be made clear by the use of such terms as 'new wool' and 'reclaimed wool'. The latter term refers to a product which may have been used several times and as a result the performance will be nowhere near as good as the new product.

Q 9

Applying knowledge Organizations exist to promote the use of natural fibres. They are concerned, to some extent, with performance factors. Examples are the International Wool Secretariat, the Cotton Institute, and the Silk Institute. The activities of the International Wool Secretariat are perhaps best known. They issue a label to indicate that the product is pure wool. This also guarantees that the wool used in the particular product is new wool and not wool which is being reused.

40

Certification Trade Mark

Pure new wool

4.3
WHAT IS TOP OF THE LEAGUE?

Main ideas in this section

The use of man-made fibres has increased rapidly in the developed countries.

Some natural fibres continue to be important despite this.

A correlation exists between the usage of man-made fibres and the degree of economic development in a country.

The purpose of this section is to show that even amongst the fibres which are chosen for clothing and household textiles, there are wide variations in their relative importance. This section is not intended to produce vast numbers of statistics for rote learning.

Q 10 and Q 11

Communicating (speech) Most pupils will probably guess cotton, but what may surprise them is that in World terms cotton accounts for approximately 50 per cent of fibre usage.

Figure 4.5
This reminds pupils that many people in the Far East almost always wear clothes made from cotton.

Figure 4.6
Although cotton is widely used in Western Europe and the United States, the percentage of cotton used is considerably different when considered in World terms.

41

This is a useful exercise in the interpretation of visually presented statistical data. These are the most important conclusions:

a Cotton remains important, but its usage is less significant in Western Europe and the U.S.A. than in the rest of the World.
b Man-made fibres, particularly synthetics, are much more important in Western Europe and the U.S.A. than they are in

the rest of the World.
c Wool usage is very small in World terms, but relatively important in Western Europe and the United States.

Figures 4.7 and 4.8
The growth in the use of synthetic fibres has been enormous when it is considered that it has taken place in less than fifty years, as *figure 4.7* shows.

It is important to use the charts in *figure 4.6* (which only show percentages and not quantities) in conjunction with *figure 4.8*.

Since 1938, far from a decrease in production, the amount of cotton used has actually increased. This is why the World's cotton manufacturers have not gone out of business. The use of synthetic fibres (from nothing in 1938) has increased considerably more rapidly, so that their usage in the United States

now exceeds that of cotton. The World's synthetic manufacturers have boomed in terms of quantity produced, although not always in terms of profit. This is because although the increase in polyester usage, for example, has been dramatic, it has not been as great as was at one time predicted. Fibre manufacturers built plants to accommodate the predicted demand. Because this was an overestimate, they produced surplus capacity which reduced their profitability.

The interesting point that *figure 4.6* shows is that synthetic fibres are more widely used in developed than underdeveloped countries.

Q 13
The reason here is partly that only a developed country has the money and technology to build the factories to make the fibre, so naturally they would be the first to use them.

Another reason is that the properties of synthetic fibres (such as being easy-care) require the benefit of technology to bring out their full potential (*e.g.* automatic washing machines).

When synthetic fibres were first introduced they were rather expensive. This again led to greater acceptance in developed countries. In relative terms the price of synthetics has fallen until most are now about the same price as cotton and some-what cheaper than wool. As a result, their use is spreading in increasing quantities all over the World.

Extension work
Pupils could consider why wool is used primarily in developed countries. The answer is that it sells very much on its aesthetic value particularly now that synthetic fibres are available with high performance. Wool is relatively expensive and is therefore much more in demand in developed countries. From this it is obvious that the two main fibres of the World for clothing and textile items are cotton and polyester. The other fibres, wool, viscose, nylon, acrylic, acetate, triacetate, and silk are at a much lower level, some of them considerably lower. These figures are on an overall basis; for individual garments or parts of garments a fibre with a low overall usage may be very important. Examples of this include wool and acrylic in jumpers and silk in certain small items, like headscarves and ties.

Predicting the future is always difficult: an interesting class discussion could take place on what the trends are likely to be. The availability of oil is an important factor in the production of synthetic fibres, but the chemicals required for synthetic fibres may be obtained from other sources, by the year 2000, possibly from coal.

4.4
ANOTHER BIG DIFFERENCE BETWEEN FIBRES: PRICE

Main ideas in this section
The price of a fibre is related to its supply and demand.

Demand may be related to whether the fibre fulfils certain aesthetic or performance factors.

Identifying causes

It will be obvious to the pupils that because price is one of the three factors involved in choice, and fibres are at the beginning of the chain, the price of a finished garment or textile item must be related to the price of the fibre. Some consideration of what affects fibre price is appropriate without entering into a wide-ranging discussion of economics.

Q 14
The fibre price consists of the cost of production plus the profit to be made. The cost of production will obviously vary. For example, wood pulp is cheap and so viscose and acetate will tend to be cheaper to produce than silk, which depends on the spinning capacity of the slow growing silkworm and its one source of food — the mulberry leaf. On top of this, other factors may affect manufacturing costs. Climatic conditions can affect the growth of natural fibres. Variations in supply

Assessing (relevant factors)

sources and energy needed to run man-made fibre factories can change costs. An obvious example is a change in oil prices.

Identifying
causes

When it comes to the selling price, the fibre manufacturer will clearly try to maximize his profit. Even if one fibre costs more than another, it can still command a better price if it has aesthetic and performance properties which make it attractive. For example, if silk did not have some advantage over viscose, it would not sell. Silk does have some performance advantages over viscose, but more importantly, it has aesthetic advantages. People will pay for these. If people really want something, and have the money, they will pay a lot more than just the difference in the cost of production. In addition, a fashion demand can add to the attractiveness of a particular fibre at certain times.

Figure 4.9
When denim jeans became a fashionable item for people all round the World in the early 1970s, the price rose several times over even though they were just the same garments as were sold as work-wear only a few years previously. To an economist this is the fundamental problem of supply and demand. If there is a short supply and a big demand then the price rises. The opposite applies when an over-supply leads to a fall in price.

Q 15
This question gives some simple examples of the workings of supply and demand.
a Bad weather increases the cost of cotton production and produces a shortage. As demand is high, the price rises.

Communicating
(speech)

b Bad weather again increases the cost of wool growing leading to a shortage. If there is a demand for winter clothing, as usually happens, the shortage forces the price up.
c The increased cost of oil increases the cost of many synthetic fibres, but a general drop in demand for clothing may keep prices down.

Extension work
Ask pupils to look at current news items and current fashion predictions to see whether the way in which fibre prices might move can be predicted. If a record is kept, these can be checked later in the year or even the following year.

Using
references

Table 4.2
The unpredictability of events is why *table 4.2* can only be a guide. The table only relates to production costs. Already, at the time of writing, the Chinese are beginning to export silk at lower prices than they used to so that they can obtain Western currency to buy some of the goods they need (such as aeroplanes). At any time, climatic conditions could affect the

price of cotton or wool. If the price of wool rises then the price of acrylic also rises. This is because acrylic can be used as a substitute for wool. However, because most people prefer wool to acrylic, the price of acrylic is unlikely to exceed the price of wool.

Extension work
Pupils can make a table of the fibres giving relative ratings to aesthetics, performance, and price. They can then suggest which is likely to be the most important factor in determining the use of the fibres.

This brings the pupils back to aesthetics, performance, and price. It reminds them that the use of a fibre is its ability to satisfy these three factors. An example of a completed rating table is given below.

Table T4.1

Fibre	Aesthetics	Performance	Price
cotton	acceptable (particularly comfort)	moderate	medium
wool	good	moderate	high
silk	very good	moderate	very high
viscose	low	low	low
acetate	low (although can imitate silk)	low	very low
triacetate	average	moderate	medium
nylon	acceptable only	good	medium
polyester	acceptable only	good	medium
acrylic	low, but used as a substitute for wool	moderate	medium

From table T4.1 it can be seen that the most important factor is aesthetics. A high-priced fibre generally has outstanding aesthetic factors. A fibre such as nylon, which is not noted for outstanding aesthetic qualities, but is favoured for its performance, can also command a high price.

Ideas for homework
Pupils could find out where the fibres in question 1 come from and what they are used for.

Concepts and skills	Pupils may be able to:
4.1 *Many are known — few are chosen* Properties of fibres. Classification of fibres. *Science/maths* Fibre structure; significance of the cross-section of fibres in relation to length. Applying knowledge, Deciding criteria, Communicating (writing), Suggesting hypotheses, Identifying causes, Classifying.	Understand the mathematical concept of the ratio of cross-sectional width to length as it relates to fibres. Suggest how they may vary in their handle. Identify correctly a variety of natural, regenerated, and synthetic fibres.
4.2 *Generics and others* Generic and brand names. Supply and demand. Economics of production. *Science/maths* Fibre production. Applying knowledge, Classifying, Communicating (writing and speech), Reasoning logically, Deciding criteria.	Recall that the generic name identifies the type of fibre and that the brand name identifies the manufacturer. Identify brand names correctly in a table. Discuss factors affecting the economic production of fibres and explain why fibre production is internationally based.
4.3 *What is top of the league?* Variations in type of fibre. Supply and demand. *Science/maths* Textile technology. Statistics. Analysing data, Assessing (relevant factors), Identifying causes, Communicating (speech and writing).	Recognize correctly the international variation in the use of natural and man-made fibres. Suggest explanations such as geography, supply and demand, and availability of technology. Identify oil as a finite resource. Suggest advances in chemical research for sources of fibres. Discuss possible future trends and make suggestions.

Concepts and skills	Pupils may be able to:
4.4 *Another big difference between fibres: price* Price related to supply and demand. *Science/maths* Statistics. Textile technology. Identifying causes, Using references, Communicating (speech).	Recognize the relationship between fibre availability and price. Relate this to style and fashion. Explain how certain factors, such as weather or fashion trends, can affect the cost of clothes.

Ask pupils to find out the location of three factories making synthetic fibres.

Find a picture of a person wearing a garment made from each of the main fibres. Ask pupils to say whether the fibre used was advertised under a generic name or a trade name.

The Background reading in this chapter describes how silk came to be known throughout the World from its origins in China.

CHAPTER 5

Producing the natural fibres

This chapter is concerned with the production of natural fibres. The most important thread which runs through this chapter and the next is the way in which the production of man-made fibres has been developed by copying the method of production of a natural fibre.

This chapter deals with the production of cotton, wool, and silk. The purpose here is not to state in detail the zoological and botanical facts relating to these fibres but simply to summarize their method of growth and the way in which the individual fibres are obtained from the plant or animal and then to use the principle to pass on to a consideration of man-made fibres. Some attention is paid to chemical structure and also to factors affecting quality and price so that the relationship to the three factors, aesthetics, performance, and price, is not lost. Pupils may have learned about the production of natural and man-made fibres in Chapter 19 of *The Basic Course*.

Time allocation
Section 5.1: 40 minutes; 5.2: 40 minutes; 5.3: 40 minutes.

Extension work in this chapter
Section 5.1: finding the average length of natural fibres.

Worksheet and Assessment card Masters
FM23   Assessment card

5.1
FROM PLANTATIONS AND GREEN FIELDS

Main ideas in this section

World production of cotton and wool is subject to various factors which cause variations in quality and production.

Cotton and wool are staple fibres.

Detailed examination of wool and cotton can reveal some of their properties.

Communicating (speech) The start of this section relates back immediately to section 4.3 and the importance of cotton. This is not a detailed biological approach to cotton growing. Nevertheless you could digress into economic geography in relation to the production of cotton. In some schools it may be possible to link with geography and other lessons.

Figure 5.1
This shows the areas of the World where cotton is grown. The Equator and the Tropics are indicated.

Q 1

Assessing
(relevant
factors)

This is not only interesting from a geographical point of view, it also links up with ideas, developed later on in this section, about quality and cost. Cotton needs a warm humid climate, or at least a warm climate with adequate irrigation. The essential requirements are a frost-free period of 6 or 7 months with mild temperatures and about 12 hours of sunlight each day. If adequate irrigation is not available, at least 3 to 5 inches of rain per month is needed, followed by a dry season when the fibres are maturing. If any of these conditions fail the cotton crop will suffer. There will be a shortage of cotton on the World market and the price will rise.

Figure 5.2
This shows the growing of cotton. The cotton plant suffers from attack by numerous pests of which the best known is the boll weevil.

Figure 5.3
This shows the harvesting and processing. Cotton is now almost entirely picked by machine in the large producing areas, but it was formerly picked by hand (hence the slaves). Hand picking actually gives a more uniform and better quality cotton because the pickers can select the mature fibres only. However, the cost of labour is now such that hand picking would be totally uneconomic in all but the poorest countries.

Figure 5.4
This repeats the approach used for cotton for wool. By comparing the areas where sheep are grown predominantly with those for cotton the generally colder climates required can be appreciated.

Figure 5.5
This gives a British illustration of the importance of wool to a society.

Figure 5.6
This looks at the production of wool.

Assessing
(relevant
factors)

One other natural fibre is not considered in this book in detail because of its diminishing importance. This is linen, which is derived from the flax plant. Its origins date back into history. It may indeed be the oldest fibre used in the Western World. Fragments have been found at Swiss lake villages dating back to 10 000 B.C. The former importance of linen in the economy of

Northern Ireland should be considered. Nowadays the main producers are the U.S.S.R. and Belgium. Retain some interest in linen so that the reason for its decline in popularity might be considered based on later knowledge of fibre properties. As a start you could tell the class that linen requires three times as long to mature from planting to the fibre-ready stage as does cotton.

EXAMINATION OF RAW WOOL AND COTTON FIBRES

This investigation is intended to ensure that the pupils know what a staple fibre is. They should be able to note the variation in length between fibres in a batch of the same fibre. The crimp in wool will also be observed.

You will need for each pair or group of pupils
Raw cotton fibres   Hand lens
Raw wool fibres   Dissecting needle
                                          Ruler

Practical
skills

Observing

Do not give out too great a quantity of raw fibres. There should be just enough to extract the 10 fibres required later. Encourage the use of the naked eye first and then the hand lens to show the greater detail which can be seen.

Q 2
At this level of magnification structural differences between the fibres will not be seen (for instance the scales on wool will not be apparent). Both fibres will be long and thin. Pupils may notice that the wool fibres are generally longer than the cotton.

An important difference should be the crimp. Measuring the fibres may present some difficulty, but it provides a good exercise in manual dexterity in that fibres have to be held up against a ruler.

Measuring

Q 3
The longest wool fibre should certainly be considerably longer than the longest cotton fibre. A likely length of wool is about 15 cm but it can be up to 30 cm. For cotton it is likely to be about 4 cm with a maximum of 6 cm.

Q 4 and Q 5

Assessing
(relevant
factors)

Observing

Measuring

With a reasonable sample, cotton fibres can be as short as 1 cm and wool about 3 cm, and there should be variations between the shortest and the longest fibres. There will obviously be a variety of answers within the class. Although wool and cotton differ in length on average, they are both relatively short and the term *staple fibre* should be clearly understood. Because wool is generally longer than cotton, the trade does distinguish between long and short staple. When man-made fibres are produced to blend with natural fibres they are produced in long and short staple form to blend with the appropriate natural fibre.

Extension work

Estimating

Pupils could gather 10 fibres at random and measure them. This could be done for both cotton and wool. Examining the 10 results for each fibre type will give a further illustration of the variations in fibre length to be found. Pupils could then be asked

Analysing
(data)

to calculate the average fibre lengths for cotton and for wool using the following formula.

Average length of fibre =

$$\frac{\text{total lengths of sample fibres}}{\text{number of sample fibres}}$$

Although some cotton fibres may have been found that are longer than wool fibres, on average wool will be longer than cotton. As an additional exercise, a distribution curve could be plotted showing the spread of fibre lengths between the shortest and the longest.

Link with school maths

Pupils should have covered work on averages by the age of thirteen.

The variations between the fibre lengths are all part of the problem of natural fibres. This can be stressed now so that it can be compared with the careful control of length and quality which is possible in man-made fibres. There is no need to go into great detail about the great variety of cotton and sheep that are used unless particular interest is shown. The main point is that they do exist largely to cope with climatic variations and because they exist there are variations in fibre quality. Nonetheless these variations can be very interesting. For example, the Merino sheep which originated in Spain was kept a closely guarded secret but finally the secret was lost. Spain now has virtually no wool production but the Merino sheep is used all over the World. Two new breeds of sheep have been derived from the Merino called the Delaine and the Rambouillet. These wools are slightly coarser but of very good quality. The coarser wools come from such sheep as the Navaho, Cotswold, Lincoln, and Romney. Notice how many of the names are British in origin. This is also true of the medium type of wool which comes from such breeds as Cheviot, Corriedale, and South-down.

Figure 5.7

This shows a typical sheep used for coarser wools. The term crossbred generally implies that the sheep is used for both meat and wool production.

5.2
THE USEFUL MOTH

Main ideas in this section

The production of silk depends on a moth.

Silk is a filament yarn.

Communicating (speech) Pupils may ask why silk is introduced here, since its use is very limited. There are two reasons. Partly it can be justified on the commercial grounds that its use is increasing and is likely to continue to do so because of the availability of relatively cheap supplies from China. Secondly, understanding the method of production of fibre by the silkworm is necessary to illustrate the method of production of man-made fibres. Silk has a long history largely connected with China.

Figure 5.8
This shows the main areas where silk is produced.

Figure 5.9
This gives the life cycle of the silkworm and method of production. Stress the reliance of silk on the availability of the mulberry tree. Production of silk only takes place where mulberry leaves are available.

EXAMINATION OF SILK FIBRES

You will need for each pair of pupils
Silk fibre sample

Hand lens or microscope

Practical skills

Observing

Assessing ideas

Pupils look at a filament yarn or fibre, as opposed to the staple fibres examined in section 5.1. This is brought out in question 6. Note that when the silkworm extrudes the liquid fibre from its spinnerets it actually has two tiny orifices in its head (see *(figure 5.9)*. It therefore theoretically spins a two-filament yarn. However, it is generally impossible to distinguish these two filaments as they bond together as a single (mono-) filament on extrusion. Silk, when wound, is made up of a number of these mono-filament yarns produced by the silkworm, and is a multi-filament yarn. It should be clear from this section what the difference is between a filament fibre and a staple fibre. The problem of whether to use the term fibre or yarn largely relates to the textile trade. The fibre industry tends to use the term fibre but the spinning industry tends to use the term yarn.

Mono-filament yarn is produced. Two examples are: a type of sewing thread and a filament which is cut up and used for toothbrush bristles.

Concepts and skills	Pupils may be able to:
5.1 *From plantations and green fields* Staple fibres. Cotton. Wool. Fibre structure. *Science/maths* Chemical structure of fibres. Botany. Zoology. Averages. Magnification. Observing, Measuring, Communicating (diagrams, speech and writing), Applying knowledge.	Distinguish between cotton and wool fibres. Note details of structures, variation in shape, appearance, and length. Know the term 'staple' fibre. Explain why the quality of natural fibres varies.
5.2 *The useful moth* Mono- and multi-filament fibres and yarns. *Science/maths* Extrusion. Structure of materials. Magnification. Applying knowledge, Communicating (speech and writing), Practical skills.	Give examples of natural fibres, stating whether each is a staple or a filament yarn. Recall that staple fibres are short fibres and that filament yarns can be very long (continuous). Explain how silk is produced and describe the economics of it.
5.3 *The building blocks of fibres* Chemical structure of fibres. Polymers. *Science/maths* Giant molecules. Cellulose. Proteins. Polymerization. Applying knowledge, Communicating (speech and writing), Reasoning logically, Using references.	Recall that cellulose is the building block of cotton. Recall that proteins are the building blocks for wool and silk. Explain that a monomer is a single unit and that polymers are several identical units joined together. Explain that millions of cellulose molecules make up a cotton fibre. Explain that the molecular arrangement can vary creating different types of cellulose.

Assessing
(relevant
factors)

This examines the whole question of cost in relation to
seri-culture. Mulberry trees do not grow easily in Britain, and
cheap labour is not available. There are only a few silk farms in
the United Kingdom. The production of silk has never been a
big industry in the United Kingdom although there was once a
thriving silk fabric industry around Macclesfield.

5.3
THE BUILDING BLOCKS OF FIBRES

Main ideas in this section

Fibres are chemical compounds all of which are polymers.

Polymers have molecules of the right shape for fibres.

Fibres produced artificially require polymers.

Communicating
(speech)

Applying
knowledge

This leads to the idea that fibres can be man-made. The explanation of how the cotton plant produces cotton need only be
done in general outline. The process of photosynthesis may well
have been covered in science lessons. The important conclusion
is that cotton is a chemical compound known as a polymer.

The polymer in cotton is cellulose, which is built up of the
molecule glucose. It should be easy for the pupils to visualize
how a long chain polymer has the same shape as a fibre. This
could be illustrated in class by beads on a string — each bead
representing the basic unit of the polymer.

Figure 5.10

Communicating
(diagrams)

This shows how the molecules build up to become a fibre. The
pupils should realize that although the molecules have the shape
of a fibre they are not the whole fibre. Many millions are
required to make one fibre and they may not actually be
arranged in parallel in the fibre. A common error at this stage is
to say that a molecule, cellulose, which is made up of glucose, is
a cotton fibre. It is not. A cotton fibre is made up of many
millions of such molecules, but their general shape enables the
traditional fibre shape to be produced. In a similar way wool is
a polymer, but this time a protein polymer. There are many
types of protein. This can be related to *Food science* and
Nutrition. Point out that wool and silk are both proteins but
they are different from each other.

Q 8

Applying
knowledge

Man-made fibres are made from polymers which are not proteins
or carbohydrates. These are just examples of polymers which
happen to be fibre-forming. Now lead on to the next stage.

Having got the correct chemical compound (which could be
one of quite a number), how do we get the shape? This is
developed in the next chapter.

Ideas for homework
Pupils could find out about the growth and decline of the
textile industry in Lancashire. They could use the financial
papers to find out current prices of fibres on the World market.

Alternatively, they could investigate the importance of silk in
the Asian sub-continent.

The Background reading at the end of the pupils' text describes
attempts on the World records for making various woollen garments. Pupils could be asked to describe the stages in the making
of, say, a cotton garment and to guess how long construction
might take at top speed.

CHAPTER 6

Man imitates nature

The previous chapter introduced the idea that a fibre requires a polymer and a means of generating a fibre shape from that polymer. This was based on the natural fibres. The principle is now applied to man-made fibres. Starting with viscose derived from a natural polymer, the modification of that natural polymer to give acetate and triacetate, and then the production of synthetic polymers whereby nylon, polyester, and acrylic are made. Finally methods of identifying and distinguishing between the fibres are considered.

Time allocation
Sections 6.1, 6.2, and 6.3: 40 minutes; 6.4, 6.5, and 6.6: 80 minutes; 6.7: 80 minutes, plus another 80 minutes for looking at fibres under a microscope.

Extension work in this chapter
Section 6.4: producing nylon.
Section 6.7: examination of fibres in cross-section.

Worksheet and Assessment card Masters
FM4 How do fibres react to burning?
FM24 Assessment card

6.1
FIRST STAGE: PRODUCE THE SHAPE

Main idea in this section

Man-made fibres can be made from natural or synthetic polymers by copying the action of the silkworm.

Assessing (relevant factors)

Pupils are reminded about the different methods of production of natural fibres. Clearly there are differences. Refer back to *figure 5.9d* which shows the two spinnerets of the silkworm.

Q 1
Do not gloss over the possibility of a man-made fibre being produced by imitating the action of a growing plant or a growing animal. However, all pupils should realize that this is very difficult to achieve artificially.

Reasoning logically

Having seen that the action of a silkworm is the best to copy, it is interesting to note that the Chinese thought of the idea about

4000 years ago but did not develop it. Remind them of other scientific inventions which were thought of a long time ago (*e.g.* helicopters by Leonardo da Vinci), but then were not produced for some centuries because engineering techniques were not good enough. This shows how one branch of science depends on another.

6.2
REGENERATING THE NATURAL POLYMER

Main ideas in this section

A suitable polymer must be found.

The polymer used to make viscose is cellulose. Viscose is therefore similar to cotton.

This section builds up to the way a man-made fibre might be produced. The two main problems have now been isolated: finding a polymer and producing the right shape. Ask pupils what criteria are likely to be important in selecting a polymer. They may suggest that it should be readily available and cheap. This is reasonable as a first step and, indeed, was what happened. But make the point that a natural polymer which could be converted into a fibre with very superior properties need not necessarily be cheap provided it gives a fibre superior in the balance of aesthetics, performance, and price to what is available elsewhere. However, there is a readily occurring polymer, cellulose, which is relatively cheap.

Q 2

This asks what form the polymer should be in, bearing in mind that cellulose is found in plants. To imitate the silkworm the cellulose must be made into a liquid, but make the following distinction in scientific terminology. This does not mean that cellulose is melted to give a liquid in the same way that ice is melted to give water. This would not be possible as heating cellulose causes it to burn. The cellulose is put into solution, that is, it is dissolved in a chemical. Again, this chemical should be readily available and cheap, or one that can be recovered during processing. This solution can then be forced through a spinneret, copying the action of a silkworm.

Figure 6.1
This shows the man generally believed to have first done this. Chardonnet was a Frenchman who discovered how to dissolve cellulose but the method he used produced nitrocellulose which was highly flammable if not explosive. His method of making viscose is now of historical interest only. The process generally used is that of Cross and Bevan.

Figure 6.2
This shows the process used for producing viscose by their method. The process is still used all over the World and in this country by Courtaulds. Because the method of fibre production involves the regeneration of cellulose, this type of man-made fibre is often called regenerated fibre.

The difference between viscose and cotton is very important. The pupils should not be confused into thinking that because viscose and cotton are different fibres they have a different basic chemical structure.

Q 3

The answer that is required here is that shorter molecules will lead to lower strength. Clearly the strongest part of the fibre is the molecule itself which requires a great deal of energy to break it. If the molecules are shorter they will not adhere together to the same extent, since the forces of adhesion are less than the forces between the atoms in the molecule. The total energy, therefore, required to break the fibre is less if there are fewer chemical bonds.

6.3
CHANGING IT A BIT

Main ideas in this section

A natural polymer can be modified to produce new fibres.

Acetate and triacetate are made like this.

There is a further logical step. Viscose is a kind of artificial cotton. Its basic chemistry is the same as cotton and therefore many of its properties will be the same, but it is not quite as good. New fibres are produced from it with a different combination of aesthetic, performance, and price factors. These are acetate and triacetate. Handling samples of acetate, triacetate, and viscose will show some of the differences between them, in aesthetic terms. Further performance differences will appear later. Make sure that the distinction is drawn between the wet spinning method for viscose and the dry spinning method for acetate and triacetate.

Figure 6.3
This shows the processes used for producing acetate and triacetate.

6.4
SYNTHETIC POLYMERS

Main ideas in this section

As a final stage in producing new fibres, a totally new synthetic polymer can be produced.

Nylon, polyester, and acrylic are examples of this.

The easiest way of obtaining a polymer for man-made fibres is to use a cheap readily available natural polymer, but the fibre produced is not as good as natural products, so new polymers have been made which give fibres superior in some ways to natural products. Synthetic polymers need not be cheaper than their natural competitors. In the early days of synthetic fibres they cost more than cotton and wool but were cheaper than silk. With increasing bulk and reduced cost of production the price of synthetic fibres has dropped substantially below that of wool and even in some areas below that of cotton. Stress the importance of oil as a source of the chemicals for making these synthetic polymers. This can be linked with chemistry lessons. Re-emphasize the question of what happens when the oil runs out. (The word synthesis means joining together, but in this context it is only applied to those fibres made from polymers built up from very simple chemical compounds.)

Figure 6.4
This simple diagram shows how a polyester polymer is built up.

The production of nylon is a very interesting story. Carothers and his team were set the problem of developing synthetic fibres by the du Pont Company in the United States. They investigated chemical methods of producing polymers which could be used. During their experiments they went part of the way to producing polyester but abandoned the experiments for the then more attractive route towards making nylon. The British chemists Whinfield and Dickson, working at Calico Printers in Lancashire, took up the task where Carothers and his team had left off, and produced polyester fibre. In the long term polyester may prove more valuable than nylon, although they are in many ways complementary.

Q 4

Applying knowledge

This is phrased in this way to see if the idea of polymerization involving two compounds shown in *figure 6.4* has been comprehended by the pupils. The answer is of course:

Communicating (diagrams)

C—D—C—D—C—D—C—D- etc.

Extension work
If chemicals are available from the science laboratories the production of nylon can be simply demonstrated without the need for fume cupboards.

You will need for this demonstration
2 ml adipyl chloride (hexanedioyl dichloride), 5 % solution in carbon tetrachloride (tetrachloromethane)
2 ml hexamethylenediamine (hexane-1, 6-diamine), 5 % solution in aqueous sodium hydroxide

5-ml beaker
Teat pipette
Forceps
Glass rod

Link with school science
Some O-level chemistry courses contain work on making nylon or a number of other plastics.

Prepare a 5 per cent solution of hexanedioyl dichloride (adipyl chloride) in tetrachloromethane (carbon-tetrachloride), and hexane-1, 6-diamine in dilute aqueous sodium hydroxide. Place a small quantity of the hexanedioyl dichloride solution in a beaker and add, by means of a teat pipette, an equal volume of the hexane-1, 6-diamine so that it floats on the top. *Do not mix the solutions.* With a pair of forceps grip the nylon formed at the interface, withdraw it and coil it on to a glass rod. If the rod is carefully rotated the nylon can be drawn off as a thin yarn. Because the polymerization does not occur under ideal conditions, and in the absence of a catalyst, the molecular chain length is too small to allow the fibres to be drawn.

Acrylic fibres also contain small parts of other polymers in what is called co-polymer formation. At this stage it is not necessary to go into further details.

The problem which was considered in question 2 arises again. How can the polymer be put into a form which can be spun? For two of the polymers the answer is different from the methods already described. Nylon and polyester do not need to be made into solutions since they can be turned into a liquid by melting, something which could not be done with cellulose. The other synthetic polymer, acrylic, would decompose if heated and so it has to be dissolved.

Figure 6.5
This shows the polyester production system. That for nylon is virtually identical. In commercial practice, nylon and polyester spinning plants are often interchangeable. If nylon demand is low, polyester can be produced on the machines in its place.

6.5
GETTING IT STRAIGHT

Main idea in this section

Spun fibres are drawn to give optimum properties.

Here a return is made to the idea that a fibre is composed of millions of polymer molecules. The molecules are not the fibres. Refer to *figure 5.10* where in cotton the molecules do not immediately line up along the length of the fibre. So it is with synthetic fibres. However there is a difference. The synthetic fibre can be drawn.

Figure 6.6
This shows the orientation of the molecules in the fibre (compare with *figure 5.10*).

Figure 6.7
This shows an idealized state which in practice is never reached. If the molecules were totally lined up in this form there would be no stretch in the fibres. Some stretch is necessary to give an ideal balance of properties. It is not difficult to see that if a fibre were pulled out the molecules might line up. Ask pupils what else is likely to happen in the fibre. It will get thinner as it is drawn, something which will be confirmed in the following practical work.

DRAWING THE UNDRAWN FIBRE

You will need for each pupil
Small sample of undrawn fibre
Ruler

Practical skills

Figure 6.8 shows how the sample should be held between the thumb and forefinger of both hands. The gap between the hands, that is, the length of the fibre to be drawn, should not be too long (2 or 3 cm).

The pupils should draw the fibre steadily apart. Moving too rapidly will result in the fibre breaking, and observations might be overlooked.

Q 5
The fibre will not extend evenly. Little nodules will be formed along its length as more tension is applied.

Q 6

Observing

The cross-sectional area decreases, *i.e.* the fibre becomes thinner. This may be difficult to observe on a fine yarn.

Applying knowledge

Designing tests

To get an accurate answer, marks should have been made on the fibre to coincide with the position of the thumbnails. It is a good exercise in devising experiments if pupils are not told this in advance. It would not be correct simply to measure the length of the fibres used, because at both ends yarn would be present which would not be drawn.

Q 8

Communicating (maths)

This is a mathematical calculation based on the answer to question 7.

$$\% \text{ increase} = \frac{\text{final length} - \text{original length}}{\text{original length}} \times 100$$

Do not give this formula initially. See if the pupils can work it out. The results of this work can be used to refer back to orientation, particularly *figures 6.6* and *6.7*. At first the fibre is as in *figure 6.6*. As it is drawn it moves closer to the orientation shown in *figure 6.7*. The little nodules are areas which remain as in *figure 6.6* when other parts of the fibre have greater orientation. This is due to localized variations in the spun yarn. When the yarn is fully extended, it will be clear that it cannot be pulled any further and hence has no stretch. This could be a desirable property. In practice, yarn is drawn to different degrees so a balance between tenacity (breaking strength) and stretch is obtained, according to the desired end use. The yarn is then fixed in this state by heat setting.

This control of fibre properties is an important difference between man-made and natural fibres. Much of the skill of a wool or cotton buyer is in spotting variations in the fibres from batch to batch. No such expertise is required when buying man-made fibres as, apart from the very rare case of human error, the fibres produced one day are consistent with those produced on any other day.

6.6
ONE MORE STAGE

Main idea in this section

Man-made fibres are produced in staple as well as filament form.

Obviously a synthetic fibre plant produces filament fibre initially. The only limitation to the length of the filament is the size of the package. The fibre is wound on different packages depending on its future use. The most usual package is that shown in *figure 6.9*.

The filament fibre or yarn is nearly always multi-filament but for different purposes the number of filaments will vary.

Applying
knowledge

Q 9

The way to increase or decrease the number of filaments in a yarn is to change the number of holes in the spinnerets (the silkworm has only two).

Now ask how it would be possible to make staple yarn. The answer is to cut up the filament yarn into the required lengths. The length will depend upon what the fibre is to be blended with (see section 5.1) or, if the fibre is not blended, what spinning system is used (see section 8.3).

Before cutting, some fibres may have crimp inserted into them artificially to facilitate blending with or imitating wool. Sarille is the brand name of a viscose staple fibre with high crimp made by Courtaulds. Although in theory both filament and staple forms can be made from all man-made fibres in practice this does not occur. Again the reason is whether or not a particular fibre in a particular form gives a combination of aesthetics, performance, and price which meets a market need. An example is viscose. For many years both filament and staple fibres were made in large quantities, but for clothing purposes the demand for filament fibre has decreased so that very little is now produced, although staple fibre viscose is still in great demand. This is detailed in *table 6.1*.

6.7
DISTINGUISHING BETWEEN THEM

Main ideas in this section

Tests can be designed to identify fibres.

Two methods are burning fibres and examining them through a microscope.

Assessing
(relevant
factors)

Suggesting
tests

The remainder of the chapter is concerned with simple tests for distinguishing between fibres. This is necessary if only to make sure that you get what you pay for at all stages in the chain of processing. Part of this section is concerned with the idea of testing rather than with the tests themselves, as an exercise in determining the validity of tests.

Communicating
(speech)

Q 10

It is fairly easy to distinguish between silk and wool, but polyester and nylon in staple form will not be distinguished easily. Even polyester and cotton may not be that easy to identify. If necessary hand out a few fibre samples to illustrate this point. Samples of dyed fabric could also be given out. In this case, even the most experienced buyers often cannot say what fibres are present. Therefore more accurate tests are often needed.

DISTINGUISHING FIBRES BY BURNING TESTS

This is a useful exercise for three reasons: it teaches experimental method and observation; it is a useful, simple test which can distinguish between many fibres; it can be used to illustrate the property of flammability.

You will need for each pair of pupils
Samples of pure fibres or small samples of pure fabric

Crucible tongs or tweezers
Bunsen burner
Flameproof mat or tray of sand

If a Bunsen burner is not available alternatives are a portable camping stove, wax tapers (definitely preferable to matches), or, probably the safest, a candle standing in a metal sand tray. All of these should be used with a flameproof mat or tray of sand.

Other precautions are as follows.

1 Use only small quantities of fibre or fabric.
2 Samples must *always* be held in tongs or tweezers, *never* in fingers.
3 Make sure long hair is tied back.
4 Loose clothing, *e.g.* scarves, must be removed or securely pinned out of the way.

To achieve the best results use undyed samples and ensure that the three instructions given to the pupils are clearly understood and carried out. This is particularly important with regard to the separate observations of the reactions approaching, in, and on removal from the flame.

You could now discuss the limitations of the test. One obvious point is that the samples are destroyed. This generally happens in chemical tests unlike physical tests (such as handle).

Q 11

Pupils should look at their own test results. Where fibres give similar results it would not be possible to distinguish between them. Cotton and viscose are examples.

The test is therefore of limited use, but it is very useful as a rough guide. It does enable certain important fibres to be distinguished, *e.g.* polyester and cotton. Further complications are the presence of dyestuffs which can mask the result, and mixtures of fibres which clearly require more detailed testing to separate them.

Fibre	When approaching the flame	When held in the flame	When removed from the flame
Cotton and viscose	does not shrink away; ignites on contact	burns quickly	continues burning; light grey ash; smells like burnt paper
wool and silk	furls away from flame	burns slowly	usually stops burning; brittle black residue; smells like burning hair
acetate and tri-acetate	melts and shrivels; may ignite	burns quickly	continues burning; hard black bead formed; acrid smell
nylon and poly-ester	melts and shrivels away from flame	burns slowly with smoky flame	usually stops burning; hard bead; polyester dark in colour, nylon lighter; acrid smell

Figure T6.1
Some specimen results.

EXAMINATION OF FIBRES UNDER A MICROSCOPE

Pupils distinguish fibres by microscopic examination.

You will need for each pair of pupils
Samples of fibres
Glycerol in dropper bottle (optional)

Microscope
Coverslips
Microscope slides

Observing

This is a more positive method of identifying fibres than the burning test. It enables most fibres to be distinguished, including the different components of mixtures.

Practical skills

The variety of synthetic fibres sometimes means that a great deal of experience is needed to distinguish between them. For detailed advice on using microscopes refer to worksheet M27.

Communicating (diagrams)

Only a very few fibres should be used if the full detail is to be seen. Avoid heavily dyed fibres.

The fibre sample can be placed on a slide only and the coverslip dispensed with. However this does not generally give very good results as the fibres will not lie flat. It is preferable to put a small drop of glycerol onto the sample on the slide and place a coverslip over it, ensuring that air bubbles are excluded. After use, the sample may be retained for some time. It may be useful to make up a set of slides before the lesson.

Longitudinal examination allows most fibres to be distinguished, but for final confirmation cross-sections are often used.

You will need
Cotton, wool, and silk fibres

Glycerol in dropper bottle
Metal plate approximately 0.5 mm
thick, with a hole drilled in it
about 0.75 mm in diameter

Pull-through yarn
Needle
Razor blade
Microscope
Microscope slide
Coverslip

Extension work
More able pupils may like to try making a cross-sectional slide. The fibres to be studied must be pulled through the hole in the metal plate. The easiest way to do this is to feed through a pull-through yarn. This serves the same purpose as a needle threader, and works in exactly the same way. Pull a bundle of the sample fibres through the hole and then, using a 'new' razor blade, slice off the fibres on either side of the hole. Put the metal plate

Figure T6.2

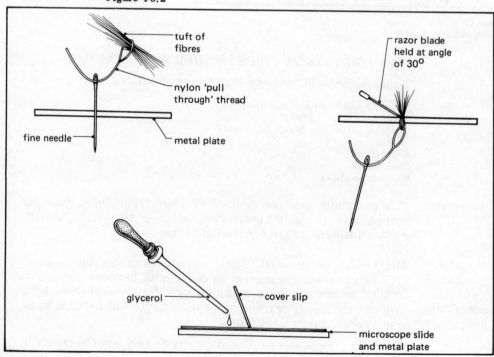

66

onto a microscope slide, add a drop of glycerol to the upper surface, and place a coverslip on the top surface making sure there are no air bubbles. View the fibres with a strong light underneath.

Cotton, wool, and silk give good results, but this is a difficult technique to perfect. Pupils may need practice before a usable slide is made.

Using the burning test and a microscope, it is usually possible to determine what fibres are present, even in a mixture. This may not be sufficient for commercial purposes when the percentage of each fibre needs to be known. The only way to do this is by a series of chemical tests which dissolve out one fibre at a time.

Ideas for homework

Applying knowledge

Pupils could be asked to design a simple pump which might be used to extrude a polymer through a spinneret.

Designing tests

Practical skills

Alternatively, they could design a test to measure the viscosity of various substances (viscosity = thickness). Note that worksheet M13 in *The Basic Course* gives instructions on measuring the viscosity of sauces.

They could investigate the use of other polymeric substances in the home and find out their chemical formulae.

The Background reading in this chapter considers the introduction of nylon. It describes how nylon became an acceptable substitute for natural fibres for a wide range of uses. Pupils could compare the aesthetics, performance, and price factors for a number of end uses where nylon has been substituted for a natural fibre.

Concepts and skills	Pupils may be able to:
6.1 *First stage: produce the shape* Polymers. Extrusion. *Science/maths* Natural polymers textile technology. Applying knowledge, Communicating (speech and writing), Assessing (relevant factors), Reasoning logically.	Recall correctly examples of natural polymers. Recall that the silkworm produces the silk polymer in its body and extrudes it through its spinnerets by muscle action. Discuss the difficulties of imitating the action of a growing plant or animal.
6.2 *Regenerating the natural polymer* Man-made polymers. Viscose. *Science/maths* Regeneration of cellulose. Chemical bonds. Applying knowledge, Communicating (speech and writing), Assessing (relevant factors).	Recall the two main problems, *i.e.* finding a polymer and producing the right shape. Explain the need to make a fibre with a satisfactory balance of aesthetic, performance, and price factors. Explain that the forces of adhesion in shorter molecules are low and that this reduces the strength of fibres.
6.3 *Changing it a bit* Modification of natural fibres. Viscose. Wet spinning. *Science/maths* Textile technology. Oil refining. Petro-chemical industry. Applying knowledge, Communicating (speech, writing, and diagrams), Reasoning logically.	Recognize that chemical modification of a natural polymer can produce new fibres. Produce a flow chart of the production processes. Compare the uses of cotton and viscose.
6.4 *Synthetic polymers* Synthetic polymer. Nylon. Polyester. Acrylic. History of nylon. *Science/maths* Giant polymers. Applying knowledge, Communicating (speech and writing), Observing.	Name the source of raw materials of polyester, nylon, and acrylic. Recognize that synthesis means building up from simple structures and how it relates to polymerization. Explain that nylon 6.6 is produced by a synthesis of two chemicals; nylon 6 from a single chemical.

Concepts and skills	Pupils may be able to:
6.5 *Getting it straight* Orientation of molecules for fibre strength. Drawing. *Science/maths* Fibre properties and control. Applying knowledge, Reasoning logically, Communicating (speech and writing, Practical skills.	Recall why fibres are drawn. Recall that the greater amount of contact between molecules the stronger the fibre. Explain why there are greater variations in natural fibres than there are in man-made ones.
6.6 *One more stage* Varying fibre thickness and length. Staple and filament man-made fibres. *Science/maths* Modifying fibre properties. Applying knowledge, Communicating (speech and writing).	Explain the difference between staple and filament yarns. Name the forms of man-made fibre used for clothing. Make a list of garments and suggest a suitable fabric for each.
6.7 *Distinguishing between them* Identification of fibres. Flammability. *Science/maths* Chemical and physical identification of fibres. Effects of heat. Observing, Classifying, Communicating (speech and writing).	Identify fabrics correctly using *figure 6.11*. Identify fibres correctly using *figure 6.12*. Suggest reasons why a positive identification may be difficult.

CHAPTER 7

Comparing the fibres

This is probably the most important chapter in the book. It looks at fibre properties in a way that will enable pupils to make meaningful comparisons between the various items of clothing and household textiles which they see offered to them by the retail and distributive trades. The whole emphasis is on comparison, unlike most textile textbooks which list properties of fibres under each particular fibre and do not make comparisons between them. Aesthetic and performance properties are considered. Finally, it is shown that no one fibre has a monopoly of desirable characteristics. From this, the idea of blending fibres to give a compromise of higher acceptability is developed.

Time allocation
Sections 7.1, 7.2, and 7.3: 80 minutes; 7.4: 40 minutes; 7.5: 120 minutes; 7.6: 80 minutes; 7.7: 80 minutes; 7.8: 40 minutes.

Extension work in this chapter
Section 7.6: further experiments in water absorption.

Worksheet and Assessment card Masters
FM3   Looking at fibres with a microscope
FM4   How do fibres react to burning?
FM5   Effect of wetting on thermal insulation
FM6   Thermal insulation for warmth
FM8   Fabric strength
FM14 Minimum-iron finish
FM15 Superwash wool
FM17 Fabric cling and anti-stat
FM25 Assessment card

7.1
WHAT TO COMPARE?

Main ideas in this section

Aesthetic properties and performance properties can be compared.

The performance properties include durability, shape and size retention, water absorption, insulation, and flammability.

Identifying causes

An important concept introduced in this section is what properties are going to be compared. Although this chapter is ostensibly about fibre properties, what really matter are the properties of the finished garment or textile item. Fibre properties alone are the concern of the first link in the chain, that is between fibre manufacture and yarn production. Similarly, yarn properties alone are of interest in the second stage of the chain — from yarn to fabric. The properties of interest to the consumer and hence to the home economist are those of the finished product. The finished product is (as shown in Chapter 2) made up of a number of finished fabrics. The performance of the finished item can be examined as the sum of the various components, of which the most important is the main body fabric.

Reasoning logically The approach in the book is to look at fibre properties, but only from the viewpoint of those properties which matter in the finished product. Chapters 8 and 9 show how these fibre properties, which must be the basis for the final properties, are changed or modified by subsequent yarn or fabric making processes. Chapter 12 considers how finishing treatments may further modify the properties. In Chapter 13 the various components are put together in a finished garment and any modification of properties which might occur is considered.

The pupils therefore build up a pattern of knowledge of textile properties which can be applied to most everyday garments and textile items.

Worksheet FM3 helps pupils identify fibres under a microscope.

Assessing (relevant factors) The section begins by reminding pupils of the important fibres. Emphasize that all these fibres are successfully sold and used in textiles. When comparisons are being made, it will be tempting to condemn some of these fibres as useless because they are clearly inferior in some performance properties to others. (Fibres are sometimes produced which are not successful because they are too inferior. Examples are the fibres derived from peanuts which were made in the 1950s.) The relative importance of some of the fibres will change, but all the fibres being considered provide a satisfactory solution to the aesthetics, performance, and price equation.

Fibres of course have aesthetic properties as well as performance properties and in reminding pupils of this reference can be made back to Chapter 1.

Q 1

Communicating (writing) This begins the process of determining which performance properties are important, based on the idea that it is the properties which matter to the consumer which must be considered. Make sure any answers distinguish between performance properties (like lasts a long time, washes easily) and aesthetics (looks good, hangs right).

Classifying	Now these performance properties can be grouped under sensible headings. One of these is durability which embraces expressions like 'lasting a long time' and 'not wearing out quickly'. It is important to distinguish between shape retention and size retention. Size retention means that the item will, after use and cleaning, still fit as it did before. This can apply to a shirt fitting at the collar, or a sheet fitting a bed. This is in a way one aspect of shape retention, but this term is generally used to imply retention of outline. To make this clear it might be possible to link up with mathematics or physics lessons. If a geometric figure is translated or rotated it keeps its size and shape; if it is enlarged it keeps its shape but not its size.
Assessing (relevant factors)	Two other properties are important and will be considered. They are water absorption and insulation. Both are related to comfort. Finally, flammability can also be considered. Pupils may mention such things as snagging or pulling; these are aspects of durability but relate to fabric structure and are not considered in detail in this book. They may also mention dye fastness; this is related to the nature of the dye as well as the fibre and is considered in Chapter 10.
Applying knowledge

Assessing (relevant factors) | Pupils may make statements like garments should 'wear well'. Try to point out that this is a vague statement since it implies not only durability but also aspects of shape and size retention. Another statement which may be made is 'washability'. Again this is a rather open term and pupils should be encouraged to see that in many ways it is meaningless. Practically every textile article is washable; what matters is whether it comes out in a condition where it can easily be made wearable or usable again. Washability involves shape, size retention, and dye fastness. |

Figure 7.1 illustrates a few problems that can arise when the performance properties are not up to standard.

7.2
HOW TO COMPARE

Main ideas in this section

When comparing materials, only one variable should be altered at a time.

What matters is how fibres perform in clothes, so fabrics should be compared rather than fibres.

For valid comparisons to be made, fabrics must be similar in construction.

Figure 6.2
This reminds the pupils of the large variety of fabrics which can be made from a single fibre, in this case wool.

Q 2

A similar list for cotton can include velvet, jersey of the T-shirt type, towelling, tent fabric, and underwear.

Deciding criteria

Reasoning logically

Designing tests

The types of fabric normally made from cotton differ quite considerably from those made from wool, but comparison between the fibres must be made on comparable fabrics. Having found any difference between the fibres it is then possible to consider the difference that construction makes. This is a logical scientific way of approaching the problem. Thus in this chapter the difference between fibres is considered. In Chapter 8 the effect that construction can give on top of this is considered.

Assessing (relevant factors)

Communicating (maths)

Assessing (validity)

There is one other important point to be made. If you are comparing something you will make judgments about it. You will say that one fibre is better than another for a particular property. This alone may not be enough. To be more accurate scientifically you may need to set up some sort of scale, perhaps a 5-point scale. Sometimes names can be attached to the points on the scale. For example, 5 is excellent, 4 is good, 3 is medium or average, 2 is poor, 1 is very poor. The danger of using words like this is that they can cease to be comparisons and can become judgments of suitability. If, for example, you say that one fibre is very poor *compared with* another fibre for a particular property, it should not be taken to mean that the very poor fibre is unsatisfactory. Indeed it may be perfectly satisfactory for some end uses. Even if it is very poor on one property compared with another, it may be considerably better for another property. Remember that all the fibres being considered are those which are in wide commercial use (see Chapter 3). The fact that they are in wide commercial use means that for a lot of people, for some end uses, these fibres satisfy the equation of aesthetics, performance, and price. An obvious example of this is acetate fibre. Many of its performance properties are poor when compared with polyester and nylon. It may not have the aesthetic appeal of silk, but it is a cheap fibre and for many end uses the combination of aesthetics, performance, and price that it gives is widely accepted.

7.3
AESTHETICS FIRST

Main idea in this section

When aesthetic properties are considered, judgments can be made but they are a matter of opinion (see Chapter 1).

COMPARING AESTHETIC FACTORS

You will need for each group of pupils
Fabric samples

<table>
<tr><td>Communicating
(writing)

Practical
skills

Applying
knowledge</td><td>The results offered will be the pupils' personal views. Handle and one or two other properties could be assessed on a 5—1 scale. Compare the class results and point out that disagreement does not imply right or wrong. You may need to make lists of words to help the pupils express their opinions. In doing this, try to use words that have some exact meaning and avoid lazy words like 'nice' or 'pretty'. The important point to bring out is that what is acceptable in aesthetics cannot be defined, unlike performance properties.</td></tr>
</table>

7.4
HOW LONG WILL IT LAST?

Main ideas in this section

Fabrics wear out because of physical and chemical factors.

Durability is a complex mixture of these factors.

<table>
<tr><td>Assessing
ideas</td><td>Everyone is familiar with fabric breakdown (holes or tears). What is not always realized is that 'wearing out' is the result of more than one factor. Some of these factors are physical. The yarns may separate from each other in the fabric, or the fibres may separate from each other in the yarn, or even break. Other factors may be chemical, where the molecule of the fibre is actually broken down. The first common physical factor is abrasion or rubbing. *Figure 7.4* illustrates this.</td></tr>
<tr><td>Communicating
(speech)</td><td>Q 3
Other places where abrasion is likely to occur are collars, shoulders where loads might be carried, cuffs, at the waist where shirts and blouses are tucked in, on the seat, knees, and the bottoms of trouser legs, on the heels and toes of socks, and the insteps of fabric shoes.</td></tr>
</table>

COMPARING THE ABRASION RESISTANCE OF SAMPLE FABRICS

<table>
<tr><td>Practical
skills

Measuring</td><td>You will need for each pair of pupils
9 sample fabrics
Cocoa tin or jam jar
Pumice stone
Rubber band or string</td></tr>
<tr><td>Identifying
causes</td><td>Although the test is very simple, try to get some level of scientific accuracy into it by standardizing the test method so that the results are comparable. Stress the importance of a slow,</td></tr>
</table>

74

regular movement with even pressure. The only difference between the method used and commercial abrasion testers, such as the Martindale, is that they are designed to exert exactly the same amount of pressure over a fixed area each time. Variations in results may be due to differences in rubbing techniques. The probable order of durability will be:

nylon, polyester   most durable
silk
wool
acrylic
cotton
viscose
triacetate and acetate   least durable

Pupils may have used a 'wear-tester' in *The Basic Course*, Chapter 19.

Assessing (relevant factors)

Other physical factors in wearing out are tensile action (pulling), tearing, and flexing. These are illustrated in *figure 7.6*. It can be seen that although all these tend to pull the yarns and fibres apart, some fabrics will be more affected by some factors than others.

Deciding criteria

Tests for physical factors test only one aspect of wearing out. In some ways more important causes of breakdown are chemical factors. Everybody knows that fibres, and hence fabrics, are destroyed by excessive heat (see section 6.7). Burning is a chemical reaction. The fibres are combining with the oxygen in the air and so the chemical composition changes. Other chemicals can also destroy fibres. Very strong acids like sulphuric acid (H_2SO_4) would harm most fibres. Wool should not be washed in strong detergent as it is too alkaline and alkali damages wool. Strong acid is not normally dropped on clothing, but we do constantly perspire. Perspiration contains chemicals which attack fibres. The fibres most affected are the natural and regenerated ones.

Finally, one of the main sources of chemical breakdown is sunlight. The ultra-violet radiation from the sun breaks down the actual fibre molecules. Once the molecules are broken, the fibres are weakened. Every fibre is affected this way, both natural and man-made.

Q 4

Communicating (speech)

Examples are curtains, upholstery and carpets near a window, beachwear, tents, and sails. The overall result is that assessing durability is difficult.

Communicating (diagrams)

Figure 7.7 gives an approximate order but remember that it is for comparable fabrics. Notice also that, compared with the table given in section 7.3, although polyester and nylon are still at the top, acrylic has moved up because it is less affected by chemical

75

degradation. Do not forget to re-emphasize the fact that low durability is comparative and may be perfectly acceptable for certain garments. A wedding dress need not last for long.

Worksheet FM4 demonstrates how finishes react to burning. Pupils should see the implications of these tests for fabrics used in home furnishings.

Worksheet FM5 considers the effect of wetting on thermal insulation.

7.5
STAYING IN GOOD SHAPE

Main ideas in this section

A textile item must not shrink or stretch permanently.

Some fabrics recover better from creasing or wrinkling than others.

Sometimes a crease or pleat may be advantageous.

Identifying causes

Communicating (writing)

Although it is usual to talk about shrinking and to assume this is the only problem to do with keeping the right size, stretching or extension can be almost as bad. Most fabrics which are unstable will shrink. Acrylics have a tendency to stretch. The usual cause of instability is poor finishing. One fibre, wool, has a built-in shrinkage problem. Relate the felting of wool to the fibre structure observed under the microscope (see section 6.7). This shows that fibre performance is not only related to chemical composition but also to its physical structure. Controlled felting can of course produce a desirable fabric and felts were once in great demand, particularly in the millinery trade. *Figure 7.8* shows the effect of undesirable felting. Wool shrinkage and its prevention are considered in Chapter 12.

Reasoning logically

A garment also loses its shape due to wrinkling or creasing. Strictly speaking this is a wrong use of words as everything must wrinkle or crease in order to be comfortable in wear (see Chapter 3). Point out that what matters is how well the fabric recovers from creasing. Although the word creasing is commonly used in the United Kingdom, it can be confusing, as sometimes garments need a crease, *e.g.* trousers. For this reason the American word wrinkle is probably better.

The pupils test the crease or wrinkle recovery of similar fabrics made from different fibres.

You will need for each group of pupils
9 fabric samples
Clock or watch with seconds hand

76

Try to introduce some scientific accuracy by standardizing as far as possible the creasing action. The points to be watched are the force with which the fabric is crumpled in the hand (there is no need to exert such force that one's knuckles turn white) and the length of time that the fabric is gripped.

In wear, creasing does not always occur under dry conditions. In any area where there is a high level of perspiration, and in washing, creasing is taking place in the wet. The results may be very different.

The pupils test crease or wrinkle recovery of similar fabrics made from different fibres when wet.

You will need for each group of pupils
9 fabric samples (the same ones as before)
Water plus a *little* detergent in a bowl

Clock or watch with seconds hand
Iron and ironing-board

Try to ensure that the tests are carried out in exactly the same way as before. The detergent is present simply to help wet the fabrics, so only a very small quantity need be used.

Q 5

The synthetic fabric should show the least difference in performance. Probable results are shown in table T7.1.

Table T7.1

Fabric	Dry	Wet
Acetate	2	1
Acrylic	4	3
Cotton	3	2
Nylon	5	5
Polyester	5	4
Silk	4	1
Triacetate	4	3
Viscose	3	2
Wool	5	2

Q 6
Any variation with pupil's experience may be due to faulty memory or because of differences in construction.

Use question 6 in conjunction with the assessed results to discuss an important aspect of all testing: 'criteria of acceptance'.

All the fabrics tested are used commercially which means that they are acceptable to somebody. If you were buying textiles to sell in a shop and trying to predict what customers would accept, what level of creasing performance would you set?

If you were going to describe a fabric as 'minimum care', what creasing standard would you require? Obviously 5 could be equated with non-iron and 1 would certainly require ironing. Where would you draw the line? These are the sort of questions which people in the textile trade need to answer.

ANOTHER PART OF GOOD SHAPE

This may be a good place to remind pupils of the confusion over the word 'crease'.

Q 7

Men's and sometimes women's trousers, pleated skirts, and vents in certain jacket styles all have creases. The application of a physical force will cause all fabrics to crease or pleat, but then they recover to some extent. The crease is generally removed by washing, although others may be put in. Certain fibres can be set under the influence of heat, particularly nylon and polyester and, to some extent, triacetate.

The pupils compare pleat retention in similar fabrics made from different fibres.

You will need for each pair or group of pupils

9 samples of fabrics	Oven (pre-heated to 160 °C)
9 sets of pleat formers	Clock
String (not polypropylene type)	Bowl of hand-hot soapy water
	Spray bottle
	Knife

There are a number of points which will help the organization of this experiment.

1 If time is short, use cotton and polyester for a good comparison.

2 It may help if pleat formers are made in advance (see *figure 7.10*). The pleats (made of thin card) should be about 1.25 cm in depth. A fabric sample of approximately 10 cm × 10 cm is required.

3 Make sure the fabric does not protrude from the sides or ends of the pleat former.

4 Do not use polypropylene string — it will melt!

5 The fabrics need wetting before placing in the formers, but make sure they are not dripping wet.

6 20 minutes should be sufficient time for the water to evaporate, but if the oven has uneven temperatures longer may be needed.

78

7 Allow the pleat former to cool before removing the fabric.
8 One way of assessing the washed sample is to hang it alongside the unwashed half. Make sure that the pleat line is parallel to the line on which the samples are hung. Those fabrics which have not retained the creasing will therefore be longer than the unwashed sample, although the samples will have come out to some degree.

7.6
WATER ABSORPTION

Main ideas in this section

Most synthetic fibres absorb little water.

Fabrics made with these fibres do get wet, but they dry comparatively quickly.

Static electricity can be a problem in fabrics with low moisture absorbency.

Assessing
(relevant
factors)

It is important to understand the mechanism by which fabrics get wet, as pupils are often confused. In principle they are told that synthetic fibres do not absorb water, but clearly after washing synthetic fibres are wet.

Q 8

Communicating
(speech)

The term drip-dry is in many ways a misnomer as everything will dry eventually in the right conditions. It means 'dries quickly' but this is only relative.

Reasoning
logically

Identifying
causes

The pupils must realize that there is a difference between the water which is trapped between the yarns and fibres in any fabric (the amount depending upon the fabric's construction) and the water which is absorbed by the fibre itself. The former will quickly run off a fabric, whereas the latter may be difficult to remove (*e.g.* drying towels). The words hydrophilic and hydrophobic are derived from the Greek and mean water-loving and water-hating. *Figure 7.12* shows how fibres differ. *Figure 7.13* shows a common application of the principle.

The pupils measure the rate of drying of similar fabrics made from different fibres.

You will need for each group of pupils
9 fabric samples
Bowl of water plus one 15-ml (table) spoon detergent

Line and clothes pegs
Tumble drier
Balance for weighing

<table>
<tr><td>Practical
skills

Observing</td><td>Dry the samples thoroughly first and weigh each sample accurately. Use a 15-cm square of each fabric (perhaps the sample used in section 7.3). Noticeable differences should appear after 5 minutes dripping, but if not, allow the samples to drip for a further 5 minutes.</td></tr>
</table>

Communicating (maths)
Use the equation given in the pupils' text to make a table, since this removes any variation due to difference in weight of the original fabric samples.

Extension work
Pupils could carry out measurements for each fabric over a period of time (say 30 minutes) at 5 minute intervals. Plot a graph for each fabric sample of the percentage of water remaining against time. (See figure T7.1.)

Figure T7.1

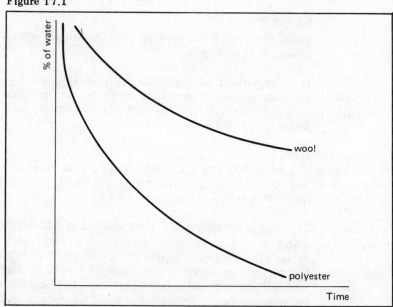

Communicating (maths and graphs)
Most people would regard quickness of drying as an advantage, so the synthetics would be highly rated. Point out that an advantage in one area can easily be a disadvantage in another. Sometimes the ability to absorb moisture is an advantage, such as in absorbing perspiration, as *figure 7.15* illustrates. In these circumstances synthetic fabrics are a disadvantage.

This illustrates in a graphic way that there is no such thing as a perfect fibre, a point which will be considered later. A further disadvantage of low water absorption concerns static electricity.

Identifying causes
Most pupils are familiar with the problem of static in clothing and household textiles and how it is possible to receive a small shock when static is built up and they touch something metal

which will conduct the charge away. All fabrics are capable of retaining a static charge if all water is removed from them. Cotton garments from a tumble drier will do this. Equally, under moist conditions, static is not a problem even with hydrophobic fibres. Worksheet FM17 explains this and shows the effect of fabric softeners.

The pupils compare the dust pick-up of similar fabrics made from different fibres.

You will need for each pair of pupils
9 fabric samples plus a sample of anti-static nylon
Loose dust from a cleaner

Practical
skills

Try to obtain fairly fine dust without too many large particles. As an alternative to dust from a cleaner, cigarette ash may be used. Ensure that no pupil is allergic to it or the dust. The experiment will not work in very humid conditions. ⚠

Observing

Q 9

Communicating
(speech)

There should be a reasonable correlation between this and water retention. Certainly the synthetic fibre samples, except anti-static nylon, should be worse than cotton, wool, and silk. Anti-static nylon may still pick up dust but it should be better than standard nylon. Anti-static nylon contains a small percentage of a polymer which absorbs water.

Worksheet FM15 introduces Superwash wool. Pupils should be able to discuss whether or not this solves all the problems of maintaining woollen garments.

7.7
KEEPING WARM AND KEEPING COOL

Main ideas in this section

Keeping warm or cool relates to methods of heat transfer.

This is largely independent of the fibres but related to the construction of the fabric.

Reasoning
logically

This explores one of the biggest folklore areas in textiles (how to keep warm). Start by asking pupils how they would keep warm. Answers might be to put on more clothes. Ask what sort of clothes. Then relate this to whether they are indoors or outdoors and what the climate is like. There may be a tendency to relate keeping warm to the old idea of putting on a wool garment, such as an overcoat, outdoors. If so, ask what would be the best protection in severe weather conditions such as a blizzard. What do mountaineers wear? The answer is an anorak, which is generally made of nylon or another impervious material with polyester quilting.

Assessing
(relevant
factors)

Heat is lost mainly by conduction and convection (see worksheet FM6). Conduction is reduced by the thickness of the insulation. The best insulator is air. The fibres are there mainly to trap air. It is less important which fibre it is, provided it does this. Wool is good because it can be built up into bulky fabrics, but polyester as used in quilting is equally as good. In fact any structures which can trap air will reduce conduction. An example is the string vest which traps air between the body and the garment outside it. The fibre does play some part of course, and if the fibre itself is a good insulator (as in thermal underwear) this will help, but thickness is more important. Thermal underwear generally has a brushed surface to increase its thickness. *Figure 7.16* shows how air is trapped in a fabric. Chapters 21 and 30 of *The Basic Course* look at insulation.

The pupils test the insulation properties of different fabrics.

You will need for each group of pupils
9 similar light or medium weight
fabric samples plus
2 heavyweight fabrics

11 boiling-tubes
Test-tube rack
Clock or watch with seconds hand
Kettle for boiling water
Thermometer (−10 to 110°C)

Figure T7.2

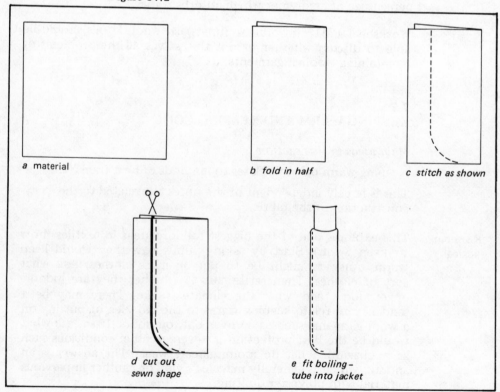

a material

b fold in half

c stitch as shown

d cut out
sewn shape

e fit boiling-
tube into jacket

Practical skills	This tests the idea of insulation as a means of reducing heat loss by conduction.
Measuring	The fabric sample should be fitted tightly around the boiling-tube by making a sleeve as shown in figure T7.2 at the bottom of the previous page.
Observing	Some pupils could make the sleeves before the lesson.
Communicating (maths and graphs)	Make sure the experiment is carried out in a reasonably draught-proof area. The number of tubes and samples handled by each pupil will depend on class ability. It might prove easier to organize if the class works in groups, each group testing one sample. Do not add water above the level of the sleeve. The temperature will fall rapidly at first, so take the first reading as soon as the thermometer registers its highest value. The type of graph likely to be drawn is shown in figure T7.3.

Figure T7.3

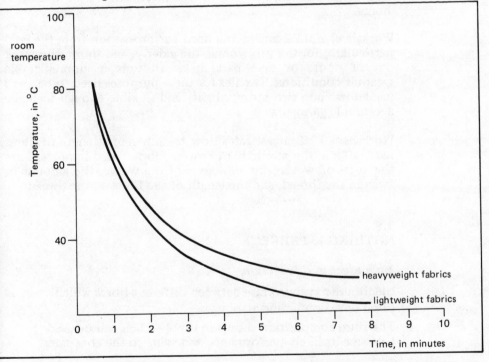

Assessing (relevant factors)	Conduction, as already mentioned, is not the only way heat is lost, and this is why this test is carried out in a draught-proof area. Wind blows through the fabric and heat is lost by convection, or to be technically accurate forced convection. This is why a string vest is useless without the garment that covers it, and why a thin nylon anorak where the fabric is coated and the wind cannot penetrate can keep you warmer than a thick

sweater which the wind will blow through. The holes in fabric are shown in *figure 7.16*.

Communicating
(speech)

Q 10

Heat loss by convection could be stopped by coating the fabric.

Worksheet FM5 will help pupils to realize that insulating textiles are useless when wet. Water reduces the thermal insulation of all fabrics because the water in the fabric is a much better conductor of heat than the air it replaces. All fabrics lose half their insulation value at only 15 per cent moisture content — which could easily be reached by perspiration alone. The sick, the elderly, and babies as well as very active people perspire a great deal. The evaporation of moisture causes further large heat losses. Synthetic fibres perform slightly better than natural ones in this respect (see down/feather on the worksheet) and will dry more quickly. Synthetics also tend to be less expensive and can be washed at home.

Worksheet FM6 explains the need for protection from the cold particularly for the very young, the elderly, and those who work out of doors or take part in expeditions in unpredictable weather conditions. Textiles for these purposes need to be good insulators, but also strong, light, and flexible enough to make acceptable garments.

Worksheet FM8 investigates how the inherent strength of fibres used affects the strength of woven fabric. Also important are the type of weave, the closeness of the weave, the amount of twist in the thread, and the length of the fibres in the thread.

7.8
NOTHING IS PERFECT

Main ideas in this section

Blends are a compromise between different fibres which often have conflicting attributes.

The fibre composition shown in textile labels can be used to assess its likely performance and value to the consumer.

This summarizes the chapter. It relates directly to the question of choice by a consumer. This choice will inevitably mean compromise.

Q 11

Assessing
(relevant
factors)

The chart should show the idea that nothing is perfect. It can be extended to give a first, second, and third ranking in each case (see figure T7.4).

84

Property	Fibre which gives the best performance
Water absorption	wool, cotton, and viscose
Durability	polyester and nylon
Shape retention	polyester and nylon
Quick drying	polyester and nylon
Anti-static	wool, cotton, and viscose
Insulation	all fibres are similar

Aesthetics are not included in the chart but can now be recalled. Here the natural fibres generally rank first. Finally, remind the pupils of Chapter 1 and the importance of price (see also section 4.4).

THE BEST OF BOTH OR ...

Assessing (relevant factors)

Try to get the pupils to come to the idea of a blend as a logical result of the differences between fabrics made with one fibre only.

Deciding criteria

You could ask pupils how they would solve the problem of polyester being very good for some things and very bad for others. They may have looked at blends in *The Basic Course*, Chapter 18.

The most popular fabrics commercially in clothing are now polyester/cotton and polyester/viscose. Explore the reasons for this. The percentage composition of the blend is important. Commercially the decision about which blend to use is difficult. A fabric made with 67 per cent polyester will not be as durable as a fabric of the same weight made with 100 per cent polyester; and 33 per cent cotton will not give the same water absorption and hence comfort as 100 per cent cotton. However, the compromise will be better than either extreme. Alternatively, 33 per cent polyester would reduce the durability too much, even though 67 per cent cotton will undoubtedly improve the water absorption and hence comfort. Not all blends are made for performance reasons. An obvious example is wool and viscose where the viscose is added almost entirely to reduce the price.

Concepts and skills	Pupils may be able to:
7.1 *What to compare?* **7.2** *How to compare?* and **7.3** *Aesthetics first* Comparative testing. Aesthetics and performance. *Science/maths:* Properties of materials. Applying knowledge, Communicating (writing and speech), Classifying, Assessing (relevant factors), Designing tests, Assessing (validity).	Identify important properties, such as aesthetics (handle and drape) and performance (durability, shape retention, size retention, water absorption, insulation, and flammability). Explain why it is necessary to compare fibres in fabrics of similar construction. Discuss the problems involved in making subjective judgments.
7.4 *How long will it last?* Durability. *Science/maths:* Physical and chemical properties of materials. Applying knowledge, Communicating (writing, speech, and diagrams), Assessing (relevant factors), Practical skills, Deciding criteria.	List the factors which can affect wear. Recognize and identify those factors which are physical and those which are chemical. Explain that accuracy can be checked by standardizing the test method. Rank polyester and nylon as most durable; acetate the least durable; and wool, silk, and cotton as of above average durability.
7.5 *Staying in good shape* Minimum care. Heat retention. Thermoplastics. *Science/maths:* Properties of materials. Effect of heat on materials. Applying knowledge, Communicating (writing and speech), Reasoning logically, Deciding criteria.	Name the fibres giving high and low performance for shape retention. Differentiate between wrinkling and wrinkle recovery. Discuss factors such as fibre type, crease recovery, behaviour under wet and dry conditions. Explain the effect of heat on a fabric's chemical and physical properties.

Concepts and skills	Pupils may be able to:
7.6 *Water absorption* Hydrophilic/hydrophobic nature of fibres. Static electricity. *Science/maths:* Water. Properties of materials, Static electricity. Observing, Applying knowledge, Communicating (writing and speech), Reasoning logically, Practical skills.	Define hydrophilic and hydrophobic. Discuss the advantages and disadvantages of the two properties as they relate to comfort, rate of drying, and static electricity. Explain that anti-static nylon contains a small percentage of a polymer which absorbs water.
7.7 *Keeping warm and keeping cool* Insulation. *Science/maths:* Heat transfer. Graphs. Applying knowledge, Communicating (writing and speech), Reasoning logically, Assessing (relevant factors), Practical skills.	State that conduction, convection, and radiation cause body heat loss. Say that structures which can trap air will insulate. Discuss quilting, bulky fabric, open mesh, and the fibre itself as methods of insulation. Describe how they work and their relative importance.
7.8 *Nothing is perfect* Blends. *Science/maths:* Properties of materials. Textile technology. Applying knowledge, Communicating (writing and speech), Assessing (relevant factors), Deciding criteria.	List properties considered when comparing fibres, such as durability, shape retention, water absorption, and insulation. Discuss the theory behind blends for a variety of textile items such as socks (wool/nylon), trousers (polyester/ wool), and bed linen (polyester/ cotton).

Q 12
See table T7.2.

Table T7.2

Blend	Reason for blend
Polyester/cotton	performance and aesthetics
Polyester/wool	performance and aesthetics
Polyester/viscose	performance and price
Polyester/silk	performance and aesthetics
Wool/nylon	performance and price
Wool/viscose	price
Wool/cashmere	aesthetics and price
Cotton/nylon	performance

Idea for homework
The Background reading in the pupils' text describes the work of the textile testing industry.

CHAPTER 8

Building up to a yarn

The next two chapters are not only meant to teach textile technology, although they are concerned with the next two stages in the clothes line: from fibre to yarn and from yarn to fabric. The methods by which this is done will be considered in technical terms, but the main point to consider is how the fibre properties investigated in Chapter 7 are either maintained or modified by processing. (Chapter 18 of *The Basic Course* looks at the difference between spun and filament yarns, and at fancy yarns.)

Time allocation
Sections 8.1 and 8.2: two lessons of 40 minutes each; 8.3 and 8.4: 40 minutes; 8.5: 40 minutes; 8.6: 40 minutes.

Extension work in this chapter
Section 8.1: mathematical estimation of the diameter of a yarn, given the number of fibres used.

Worksheet and Assessment card Masters
FM7   Spinning
FM26   Assessment card

8.1
SHORT FIBRE TO LONG YARN

Main ideas in this section

The aesthetics and performance of fibres should be retained in the yarn and the fabric.

Satisfactory yarns must be produced which can be used in the subsequent manufacturing process.

Communicating (speech) — Remind the pupils that the function of the chain of processes is to retain the properties of the fibres (both aesthetic and performance). Chapter 3 showed that the way to do this is to build up from the fibre to a one-dimensional yarn and then on to a fabric.

Deal briefly with the glue idea because it does reinforce the need to retain aesthetics and performance.

Q 1
Assessing (relevant factors) — This question follows from the rejection of glue. Clearly the only way is to lay the fibres parallel to each other, so that the friction between them holds the yarn together.

Figure 8.1

This illustrates the point that the fibre must overlap. In addition it shows how crimp in the fibre will generate bulk.

HOW IS A YARN BUILT UP FROM A FIBRE?

You will need for each pair or group of pupils
Wool fibres or cotton fibres

Tweezers
Hand lens
Ruler

Pupils lacking manual dexterity will find this exercise difficult. If this is so it may be necessary to resort to demonstration. Use a smooth flat board or surface (*e.g.* Formica), preferably in a contrasting colour to the fibres. Pick up one or two fibres at a time with the tweezers. If the fibres adhere to the tweezers a dissecting needle can be used to prise them off. When a reasonable yarn has been built up, press the fibres lightly together before measuring. Avoid draughts!

Q 2

The difference is clearly caused by the crimp in the yarn.

Q 3

It will be apparent that the answer is no.

Extension work

As a mathematical exercise, pupils can be given an average diameter for cotton and wool fibres (0.02 mm) and asked to estimate the yarn diameter. If a yarn has been made from 20 fibres, its diameter is not 20 × 0.02 mm, because the yarns are packed together in two dimensions as shown below.

Figure T8.1

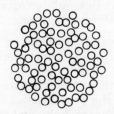

The likely diameter can be worked out by drawing this to scale, for instance by using circles of 20 mm diameter, *i.e.* 10 mm = 0.01 mm.

An estimated answer would be approximately 0.12 mm. This theoretical diameter is much less than the diameter which will appear in the experiment.

8.2
GIVE IT A TWIST

Main idea in this section

The apparent failure to produce a yarn in section 8.1 can be rectified by twisting to increase the physical contact between the fibres.

Reasoning logically

Communicating (speech)

It should be apparent that by adding twist the contact between the fibres is increased and the fibres are 'locked' together to a greater extent. If pupils have difficulty understanding this it can be demonstrated using electrical wire. Use three or four differently-coloured wires for the best results.

WHAT IS THE EFFECT OF PUTTING TWIST INTO A YARN?

You will need for each pair or group of pupils

Wool fibres or cotton fibres	Hand lens Tweezers Ruler

Practical skills

The technique of twisting the fibres together may prove difficult. If pupils cannot achieve results by lifting the sliver of fibres, it may help to roll it like dough before lifting and drawing out.

Q 4a and b

Observing

Reasoning logically

As the yarn is twisted and drawn it becomes less bulky. There is a limit to twist as some pupils will discover! Twist increases strength, but beyond an optimum point additional twist will cause kinking and the yarns finally lose strength.

8.3
COTTON, WOOLLEN, AND WORSTED

Main idea in this section

The basic method of yarn formation investigated in sections 8.1 and 8.2 is used in commercial practice.

Q 5

Applying knowledge

In the distaff spindle and the spinning wheel (*figure 8.3*) the lining-up is done by hand. In the spinning machines now used the lining-up is done in the initial carding or combing processes.

The cotton, woollen, and worsted spinning processes were evolved to cope with natural fibres; the cotton system for cotton and the woollen and worsted systems for wool. The importance of wool in the history of England is shown by the

91

fact that the name worsted derives from Worstead, a village in East Anglia. (Why the industry then moved to Yorkshire is an interesting piece of social history.)

Applying knowledge
Another spinning system known as Schappé was developed for silk. The main difference between these spinning systems was related to the length of the staple fibres (see Chapter 5). There were regional variations concerned with engineering design. In worsted spinning there were various systems such as Bradford, New Bradford, and Continental.

Assessing (relevant factors)

Reasoning logically
Man-made fibres can be made to any required length. When first developed they were cut to lengths corresponding to a particular natural fibre, and processed on the traditional systems with as little variation as possible. As man-made fibres grew in importance, especially with the introduction of polyester, the traditional systems were adapted to process the man-made fibres. The result is that the processing in spinning is now organized to maximize production of man-made yarns. One important difference is that because man-made fibres are more regular in size, contain less impurities, and are produced in a less tangled form, many of the initial stages in the traditional spinning systems concerned with aligning the fibres can be eliminated or at least reduced. When there were only natural fibres a combed yarn always gave greater alignment and therefore regularity. For 100 per cent man-made fibres, combing may be of little value as the fibres can be sufficiently aligned by carding alone.

Q 6
Communicating (speech and writing)
A difference between woollen and worsted fabrics is the relative strength of the yarns produced. When there is less fibre alignment and less twist the yarn is relatively weaker. Here is an important effect of subsequent processing on fibre properties. A polyester woollen spun yarn will not be as strong as a polyester worsted spun yarn of similar weight.

Worksheet FM7 explains how fibres can be twisted, using wool fleece and a simple spindle as an example.

8.4
WHAT A WASTE OF TIME!

Main idea in this section

Texturizing appears to be a more economical way of using filament yarn than cutting it up into staple fibres and spinning it.

Filament yarn is sometimes used in flat form. To do this it is given a little more twist than is present in the yarn when it is produced. This is known as 'throwing' and is a name derived from a similar process carried out with a silk filament.

Q 7

Silk is naturally produced as a flat filament yarn.

To achieve bulk from a flat filament yarn requires a different process. The terms bulk, bulky, and high bulk are used some-what loosely in the textile trade, as even in staple fibres the amount of bulk can be varied as has been shown with woollen and worsted. Using acrylic staple fibres with different shrinkage characteristics generates different levels of bulk in yarns.

Figure 8.5
With filament yarn the process used to produce bulk is generally called texturization.

Assessing (relevant factors)

Identifying causes

There are many yarn texturization processes. They include knife edge (Agilon), stuffer box (Banlon), air-jet (Taslan — see *figure 8.7*), knit-de-knit, and gear crimp. Commercially, by far the most important process is false twist (see *figure 8.6*). All texturization processes depend on the heat-setting characteristics of synthetic fibres. For this reason they do not work on silk, viscose, or acetate (see Chapter 7).

The most famous false twist process was that applied to ICI's polyester fibre. The texturized yarns were given the trade name Crimplene. Most people associate Crimplene with double jersey fabric which had a fashion vogue in the 1960s. The same process is now used on all polyester yarns. The texturized yarns produced are woven as well as knitted.

8.5
FLAT AND TEXTURIZED FILAMENT YARNS AND SPUN YARNS

Main idea in this section

The treatments given to filament yarns affect their aesthetics as well as their performance.

First, pupils look at the difference between flat and texturized filament yarns.

You will need for each pair or group of pupils
Sample of flat filament yarn attached to a card at one end
Sample of false twist yarn attached to a card at one end

Hand lens
Ruler

To make the comparison valid it is important to use the same basic filament yarn in both its flat and texturized form.

Q 8

Observing   The texturized yarn will stretch considerably more.

Q 9

Communicating It is important to distinguish between the amount of recovery
(writing and and the percentage recovery. The texturized yarn will recover
diagrams)   a greater amount as it originally stretched further. However,
its recovered length may be a greater percentage of its
original length than the flat filament.

Q 10

Reasoning   The texturized yarn is more bulky.
logically

AESTHETICS AGAIN

Q 11

Classifying   Fabrics must be of comparable weight and construction
for a scientific comparison.

Designing
tests   The pupils compare fabrics of similar weight made from texturized and spun polyester.

You will need for each pair or group of pupils
Sample of woven texturized filament polyester
Sample of woven spun staple fibre polyester

Q 12

Observing   Most pupils will probably like the staple spun polyester.
Remember that this is an entirely subjective judgment.

Evaluating   However, woven texturized polyester is very popular
commercially for a wide range of fabrics. It is used for
both men's and women's garments.

8.6
FANCY AND EXOTIC

Main idea in this section

A great variety of effects can be produced in yarns.

The technology is less important than the idea of how a range
of aesthetic effects can be produced. *Figure 8.8* shows simple
plying and *figure 8.9* more complex structures.

Concepts and skills	Pupils may be able to:
8.1 *Short fibre to long yarn* Yarn structure. Fibre alignment. Fibre to fibre adhesion. Bulk. *Science/maths* Properties of fibres. Adhesion. Friction. Applying knowledge, Communicating (speech, writing, and diagrams).	Recognize the relationship between fibre alignment and strength. Explain that fibre alignment creates strength in yarns by increasing contact between fibres. Explain that air trapped between fibres produces bulk.
8.2 *Give it a twist* Inter-relationship of twist and bulk. *Science/maths* Yarn structure. Surface area of fibres. Insulation. Applying knowledge, Communicating (speech and writing), Reasoning logically, Practical skills.	State that yarns are produced for different uses. Explain why high twist gives high strength and low bulk. Say that some knitting yarns are designed for high bulk, and that high bulk yarns will trap more air and so improve insulation. Describe and sketch garments and other uses for very high twist yarns.
8.3 *Cotton, woollen, and worsted* Spinning processes. *Science/maths* Properties of materials. Textile technology. Applying knowledge, Communicating (speech and writing), Assessing (relevant factors).	Name the three spinning systems (cotton, woollen, and worsted). Explain that the differences between woollen and worsted systems are fibre alignment, bulk, and twist. Describe how the term relates to the spinning system rather than the fibre content, and give examples.
8.4 *What a waste of time!* Spun yarn. Flat filament yarn. Texturization. False twist process. *Science/maths* Textile technology. Effect of heat on materials. Communicating (diagrams and writing), Assessing (relevant factors), Identifying causes.	Draw and describe the false twist process, and name some examples. Recognize that an important property is the ability of the fibre to be set by heat. Explain, with examples, that different texturization processes give different effects.

95

Concepts and skills	Pupils may be able to:
8.5 *Flat and texturized filament yarns and spun yarns* Stretch recovery properties of yarns. *Science/maths* Stretch. Percentage. Observing, Classifying, Communicating (writing and maths).	Distinguish between samples of flat filament and false twist yarns. Name the texturized yarn correctly and identify which will stretch more. Explain the mathematical relationship between stretch and recovery.
8.6 *Fancy and exotic* Core yarns and effect yarns, plying, complex structures. *Science/maths* Textile technology. Observing, Classifying, Communicating (speech and writing), Practical skills.	Recognize the basic construction of complex yarns. From given samples (*e.g.* bouclé, knop, etc.) identify the core and effect yarns. Identify fibre content by burning or examination under a microscope.

EXAMINING FANCY YARN STRUCTURE

You will need for each pair or group of pupils
Samples of bouclé, knop, two-ply yarns

Hand lens
Dissecting needles

Practical
skills
Classifying

The exercise will be easier if yarns are selected with different-coloured components. Encourage the pupils to distinguish between the core yarns and effect yarns.

Q 13a and b

Observing

Evaluating

Answers will depend on the yarns chosen. Complex yarns will obviously tend to be less hard-wearing and to cost more.

Idea for homework
The Background reading for this chapter describes the work done in the Quality Laboratory of a yarn manufacturer. It gives pupils an idea of what is involved in yarn manufacture and what jobs they might do in connection with it.

CHAPTER 9

Building up to a fabric

This chapter continues the process of building fibres up to a fabric by considering the conversion of one-dimensional yarn to two-dimensional fabric. Additionally, processes which miss out the yarn stage are considered. These fabrics are shown to have limitations although they are increasingly important commercially. (The pupils may have studied weaves, knits, and nonwoven fabrics in Chapter 17 of *The Basic Course*.)

Time allocation
Sections 9.1 and 9.2: two lessons of 40 minutes; 9.3 and 9.4: two lessons of 40 minutes (this can be less if the pupils are experienced knitters); 9.5: 40 minutes; 9.6 and 9.7: two lessons of 40 minutes.

Extension work in this chapter
Section 9.2: drafting weave patterns.

Worksheet and Assessment card Masters
FM8   Fabric strength
FM27   Assessment card

9.1
YARN TO FABRIC

Main idea in this section

The required aesthetics and performance are rarely obtained unless a two-dimensional fabric is produced.

Reasoning logically

It is important to continue with the one- to two-dimensional concept even though it may appear to be stating the obvious (*figure 9.1*). *Figure 9.2* shows a rare exception.

9.2
INTERLACING

Main ideas in this section

Weaving is interlacing at right angles.

Different patterns can be produced.

The tightness of construction also produces variations in fabrics.

The idea of weaving may be familiar to pupils. The time spent on this section and the following one will depend on their previous knowledge. It is important to ensure that the principle of weaving, that is, interlacing at right angles, is understood and the correct terminology known. (Incidentally, in the United States the weft yarn is known as the filling.)

HOW IS A WEAVE PATTERN PRODUCED?

You will need for each pupil

Yarn samples for weaving   Hand lens
4 fabric samples to copy   Old shoe box or card
Adhesive tape   Bodkin (large)

Practical
skills

Observing

Assessing
(relevant
factors)

Communicating
(writing and
speech)

Figure T9.1
An economical way of threading up the card.

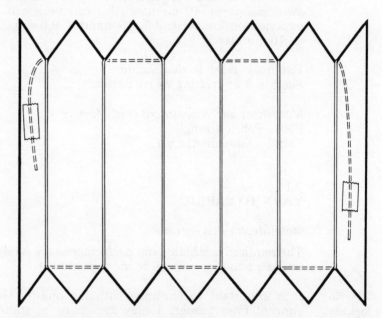

.To get a reasonable pattern, approximately twelve warp threads are needed. Since the main purpose of the practical is to examine different patterns and not to learn to weave, you could have the cards made up before the lesson. The fabric samples should, if possible, be those shown in *figure 9.6*.

Commercially, weave structure is shown by the type of diagram in figure T9.2a, where the black squares indicate that the warp yarn is on the surface.

Figure T9.2a

plain   twill

Alternatively, a pattern is built up from a series of Os or dots and crosses.

Figure T9.2b

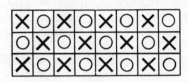

plain   twill

Extension work

Communicating (diagrams)

Pupils can extend their skills by drafting diagrams of other woven fabrics.

Identifying causes

The appearance of the fabric will also be affected by the tightness of construction. This is related to yarn size and the number of ends and picks per unit length, which is known commercially as the fabric *set* or *sett*.

Applying knowledge

The common names for fabrics are related partly to the pattern and partly to the fibre from which they were traditionally made. For instance, muslin, percale, cheesecloth, batiste, lawn, and shantung are all plain weaves. Gaberdine is a 2/1 twill. Incidentally, the term tabby for plain weave is never used commercially. Having introduced the idea of variation in construction, point out how this can affect the properties of the fabric and at times negate the properties of the fibre.

Reasoning logically

If the construction is too loose the fabric will, in effect, fall apart no matter how strong the individual fibres are. (See *figure 9.8.*)

Q 1
Slippage might happen wherever there is a point of strain: the seat, elbow, shoulder, armhole, knees, or waistband.

Worksheet FM8 looks at fabric strengths.

9.3
THE LOOM

Main idea in this section

Weaving is carried out on looms.

Observing

As with spinning systems, weaving can be dealt with in whatever detail is required. Its main purpose is to relate the principles to commercial practice.

Figures 9.9, 9.10, and 9.11

Applying
knowledge

The first stage is to set up the warp and then fill in with the weft, hence the American term 'filling'.

Assessing
(relevant
factors)

Most of the advances in weaving which have greatly speeded up the process have been in the method of inserting the weft. The traditional shuttle has been largely replaced by gripper looms (the most common is Sulzer) and by air and water jets. Before this, most advances were concerned with patterning effects, such as dobby and Jacquard looms.

9.4
LOCKING LOOPS

Main ideas in this section

Knitting is interlocking loops.

Different methods are possible (warp- and weft-knitting).

Observing

Applying
knowledge

Most pupils are familiar with 'knitting' but do not realize that there are different types. The main principle to establish is the way in which the yarn is made into a fabric, that is, by the formation of loops which are made to interlock. The difference between the various types of knitting is the way that the loops interlock and the fabric is held together. *Figure 9.14* illustrates the idea of a loop which has of itself a two-dimensional form. *Figure 9.15a* shows the principle of weft-knitting.

Weft-knitting can be carried out in a flat fabric form as in hand knitting a jumper on needles. This can be automated in the home on flat frame knitting machines. In industry it is done on similar but more sophisticated machinery, including fully fashioned machines.

Figure 9.12

A common form of weft-knitted fabric produced in industry comes from circular knitting machines. These are capable of a very high rate of production. They are used for single and double jersey and interlock fabrics, and of course, for hosiery and stocking manufacture.

The principle of warp-knitting is shown in *figure 9.15b*. Most warp-knitting machines have bearded needles, but some have latch needles. These are known as Raschel. The other types of warp-knitting machines are Tricot, Simplex, and Milanese. Of these Tricot is by far the most popular (lock knit is a fabric produced from a particular type of Tricot machine). Most of the fabrics produced on warp-knitting machines, other than Raschel, use filament yarn only. Warp-knitting is one of the fastest methods of fabric production.

HOW IS A KNITTED FABRIC CONSTRUCTED?

You will need for each pupil
Knitting wool
2 knitting needles

Practical
skills

Applying
knowledge

This activity is intended to ensure an understanding of the concept of interlocking loops. It is not a knitting exercise. If pupils are experienced knitters it can be carried out very quickly or omitted.

9.5
STRETCH

Main idea in this section
Stretch is related to method of fabric production.

Observation
v
inference

In commercial practice the choice between woven, warp-knitted and weft-knitted fabrics for a particular end use relates as usual to all three factors. Within this, stretch and hence comfort are often not the most important. Garments which need to fit closely to parts of the body are generally knitted for comfort. Discuss this with the pupils. Examples are underwear, jumpers, socks, and tights. Make them realize that usually it is only garments which are not close-fitting that are woven. Close-fitting denim jeans are quite restrictive.

Identifying
causes

In practice, structures are available which can make weft-knitted fabric as rigid as wovens. Stretch can be incorporated into woven fabrics by finishing techniques and by using elastane fibres.

COMPARING STRETCH
The pupils compare the stretch of weft- and warp-knitted and woven fabrics on the straight and on the bias.

You will need for each pair of pupils
Samples of fabrics (3 cm × 20 cm) cut in both weft and warp directions
and on the bias
Metre rule

Practical
skills
Take some care in the choice of fabrics to ensure that the weft-knit is not of a rigid structure (at least in one direction).

Q 2

Communicating
(maths)
At least in one direction, the weft-knit should give more stretch than the warp-knit, which in turn will stretch further than the woven.

Q 3

Assessing
(relevant
factors)
Reiterate the discussion on stretch at the beginning of this section.

Q 4

Classifying
There will be a considerable increase in stretch for the woven and possibly the warp-knit on the bias, but the weft-knit will probably show little change.

9.6
MISSING OUT THE YARN

Main ideas in this section

The chain of manufacturing processes can be apparently simplified by going from fibre to fabric with no intermediate yarn stage.

These types of fabrics, of which there are many, are conventionally called nonwovens, although they are very diverse.

The earliest example is probably felt. The most important types commercially are now bonded and stitch-bonded fabrics.

STICKING THE WEB

Applying
knowledge
The web can be made from different fibres. In most bonded-fibre fabrics it is either viscose or polyester and a latex (rubber) based adhesive. One of the common uses of bonded-fibre fabrics in clothing is as an interlining. The iron-on (fusible) types are coated with a material which softens under heat and sticks the interlining to the main fabric.

STITCHING THE WEB
The web is held together by rows of stitching. Again, most webs are viscose or polyester. The machines for doing this were developed in Czechoslovakia. The major manufacturers are Arachne and Mali.

HOW IS A STITCH-BONDED FABRIC MADE?

You will need for each pair of pupils
Thread (spun polyester)   Sheet of paper
Polyester fibre   Sewing machine

Communicating (maths)

The sheet of paper takes the place of the conveyor system which feeds the web to the machine in commercial practice. Try to ensure a fairly thin but even web. It does not matter how random the fibres are. The more entangled the better. For sewing methods see *figure 9.17*. The lines of stitches should be not more than 5 mm apart.

Designing tests
Measuring

Instruction 5: pupils should rub the fabric as in section 7.4; for pulling use a hand test both along and across the line of stitching. Allow the pupils to work this out.

Communicating (speech)

Q 5
The problem with stitch-bonded fabrics clearly shows how fibre properties can be affected by fabric construction. Even if the fabric is made from polyester its abrasion resistance will be low. Because the fibres are not tied up in a yarn, the action of rubbing easily separates them. This is why stitch-bonded fabrics are rarely used for clothing but do find considerable usage in curtains.

9.7
AESTHETICS YET AGAIN

Main ideas in this section

Handle and drape are a matter of taste, but the lines of stitching or adhesive produce a stiffness which many people find unacceptable.

Bonded-fibre fabrics are not used for clothing, except as interlinings.

COMPARING WOVEN AND NONWOVEN FABRICS

Classifying

You will need for each pair or group of pupils
Samples of woven and nonwoven fabrics

Practical skills

Q 6
Bonded-fibre types are used as interlinings because of their stiffness.

Applying knowledge

Q 7
Fabric dishcloths, such as J-cloths, are a type of nonwoven.

Q 8
Their low cost is an advantage.

Concepts and skills	Pupils may be able to:
9.1 *Yarn to fabric* Fabric manufacture. *Science/maths* Structures. Dimensions. Applying knowledge, Communicating (speech and writing), Reasoning logically.	State that clothing is three-dimensional and explain the term. Explain that yarns represent a one-dimensional form which must be converted to a two-dimensional form (fabric) and then to a three-dimensional form (clothing). Suggest reasons for wearing clothes made of fabric rather than just yarns, *e.g.* comfort, protection, and privacy.
9.2 *Interlacing* Weaving systems. *Science/maths* Structures. Friction. Dimensions. Practical skills, Communicating (diagrams, writing, and speech), Applying knowledge.	Draw a plain weave showing warp, weft, and selvedge. Explain with diagrams how the interlacing sequence may be varied. Say what effect yarn size and tightness of construction have on fabric weight, appearance, and slippage.
9.3 *The loom* Weaving systems. Relating principles to commercial methods. *Science/maths* Structures. Friction. Textile technology. Observing, Applying knowledge, Communicating (writing and speech), Assessing (relevant factors).	Explain that in order to weave on a loom you first set up the warp then fill in with the weft. Describe different methods of inserting the weft. Suggest reasons why different methods have been developed: technical factors, the speed of production, and the amount of labour required.
9.4 *Locking loops* Interlocking loops. Weft-knitting and warp-knitting. *Science/maths* Structures. Dimensions. Applying knowledge, Communicating (diagrams and writing), Practical skills.	Draw warp- and weft-knit structures, showing the differences in interlocking loops. Describe how variations are produced, *e.g.* by varying the interlocking sequence. Suggest reasons for the popularity of this method, such as: speed of production, the possibility of using a wide variety of yarns, non-fray, stretch.

Concepts and skills	Pupils may be able to:
9.5 *Stretch* Aesthetics, comfort in wear. *Science/maths* Structures. Dimensions. Observing, Classifying, Applying knowledge, Communicating (writing and speech), Practical skills, Assessing (relevant factors).	From given samples, identify woven fabric, weft and warp knits. Rank the woven sample as least stretchy and the weft knit as the most stretchy (at least in one direction). Suggest reasons for the differences.
9.6 *Missing out the yarn* Nonwoven fabrics. *Science/maths* Structures. Friction. Abrasion resistance. Dimensions. Applying knowledge, Communicating (diagrams and writing), Measuring, Designing tests.	Explain that nonwoven fabrics are a web of fibres held together by various methods such as adhesive bonding and stitching. Show how this may affect the properties of the fabric, *e.g.* low abrasion resistance.
9.7 *Aesthetics yet again* Aesthetics. Performance. *Science/maths* Properties of materials. Observing, Classifying, Communicating (speech and writing), Applying knowledge, Practical skills, Reasoning logically.	Identify differences between woven and nonwoven fabrics. Make a table of each fabric's aesthetic properties. Explain the limitations of nonwoven fabric for clothing; suggest uses such as interlinings and low-cost cleaning cloths.

Ideas for homework

Organizing data

Pupils could survey their own wardrobes to check which clothes are woven and which are knitted, and present their findings graphically.

The Background reading for this chapter describes the development of weaving technology during the Industrial Revolution. It provides a link with work in the history department, and there are plenty of opportunities for project work.

CHAPTER 10

Colour

In investigating the process leading from fibre to finished garment it is convenient to discuss the ways in which colour is applied to textiles by dyeing and printing. Dyeing is often thought of in relation to fabric alone, but the wide range of patterns required in textiles can only be achieved by carrying out dyeing at various different stages, depending on the pattern required. Firstly, dyestuffs are defined and the way in which colour is achieved is explained. Then the importance of selecting the correct dye for a particular fabric is considered.

Time allocation
Section 10.1: 40 minutes; 10.2: 80 minutes; 10.3: 40 minutes.

Extension work in this chapter
Section 10.2: making up and testing natural dyes, *e.g.* blackberries or onion skins; investigating the history of dyeing processes.

Worksheet and Assessment card Masters
FM9   Light and colour
FM10   Colour and fabric — mixing colours
FM11   Colour fastness of household dyes
FM12   Comparing household dyes
FM13   Colour fastness of curtain fabric
FM28   Assessment card

10.1
SUBTRACTION

Main ideas in this section

White light is made up of different colours.

The colours we see are the ones that are reflected back and not absorbed by an object.

Communicating (speech) Before this section is attempted, it is essential that the pupils understand the nature of light and its divisions into the spectral colours. (This is discussed on worksheet FM9.) The process can be a gradual concentration of ideas. Firstly recall the whole range of the electromagnetic spectrum and then concentrate on the narrow band of the spectrum which comprises visible light. Now consider the individual colour components of visible light and the division of visible light into the individual spectral colours: red, orange, yellow, green, blue, indigo, and violet. (The colours can be remembered by the mnemonic 'Richard Of York Gave Battle In Vain'.)

Link with school science
Most pupils will be introduced to the nature of light between the ages of thirteen and sixteen.

Q 1
This is of course a rainbow. In a really good rainbow there are two bows: the primary on the outside where the top colour is red and the secondary fainter bow where the top colour is violet.

Reasoning logically

Now focus upon what would happen if something could remove one or more of these colours. The way in which this is removed need not be considered at the moment — just concentrate on removing one or more of the colours. Make sure the pupils do not make the mistake of thinking that what is left if you remove, say red, is a striped pattern containing each of the individual colours except red. What is left is a *mixture* of the remaining colours. The colours remaining (*i.e.* the mixture) if an individual colour is removed are shown in table T10.1.

Table T10.1

Colour absorbed	Colour seen
Violet	yellow/green
Blue	yellow
Green	purple
Yellow	blue
Orange	green/blue
Red	blue/green

Q 2
This shifts the attention from removing just one colour leaving a mixture of the rest, to removing all the colours except one. An idea of how something appears red now emerges. If you look at a red book, for example, substances in the cover of the book are removing all the colours except red from the white light which falls on it. Red is reflected and so the book appears red. *Figure 10.1* shows this in diagram form.

Q 3
Only blue is not removed so the object appears blue.

Q 4
If nothing is absorbed then everything remains, so all the colours are reflected and the resulting mixture is white.

The process can be likened to arithmetic and a subtraction sum.
If white light is 7 (the total of all the spectral colours) then
$7 - 0 = 7$.

Q 5
This can again be approached by arithmetic. $7 - 7 = 0$. If
nothing is reflected then this means no light at all is reflected.
No light means dark, that is, black.

Worksheet FM9 considers the component colours of light. Producing a spectrum from white light is included as an experiment.

ROSES ARE RED, VIOLETS ARE BLUE
Now shift the emphasis back to the light being shone on an
object. It is important to realize that in the absence of light
there can be no colour. At night or in a dark room very little
can be seen and certainly no colours. In true darkness, such
as in a photographic dark room or underground in a cave,
absolutely nothing can be seen. Colour therefore depends on
a source of light. This can be the sun or some form of artificial
light. Everyday objects such as flowers contain substances called
pigments. These absorb part of the white light and so appear
coloured because of what is not absorbed and therefore reflected.

Q 6
A white rose has virtually no pigment, so nothing is absorbed
and everything is reflected. A mixture of all the visible
spectrum is white.

10.2
DYES

Main ideas in this section

Nearly all fibres are dyed.

The dyestuffs must be fast, and different types of dyes are
needed for different fibres.

Most modern dyes are synthetic.

Remember the importance of colour in the three basic factors —
aesthetics, performance, and price. If necessary, refer back to
Chapter 1, and remind pupils of the importance that they
attached to the right colour. The colour of textiles results from
the same principles as the colour of a rose. Textiles contain
substances which absorb some parts of the spectrum, allowing
only part of white light to be reflected back to give a colour.
These substances are not usually present in the original fibres,
but are added during processing. They are called dyestuffs.

108

These are added primarily to give aesthetic appeal, but remind pupils that aesthetics are not enough — performance is also important. The dyestuff must fulfil some performance requirements, that is, they must remain on the fabric. In other words they must be fast.

DYEING COTTON AND POLYESTER FABRICS

You will need for each pair or group of pupils

Cotton fabric, 2 20-cm squares	Scissors
Polyester fabric, 2 20-cm squares	Kettle or saucepan
Dyestuff	Washing-up bowl
Salt	Jug and spoon for mixing
Washing powder, 1 15-ml	Rubber gloves
(table) spoon	Skewer

Use a cold-water dye recommended for cotton only. Use definite colours such as red, blue, or strong pink.

The polyester must be about the same weight as the cotton, and must be 100 per cent polyester and *not* a mixture such as polyester/cotton or polyester/viscose.

Practical
skills

The idea of dyeing may be familiar to the pupils, but the purpose of this section is to establish a number of important points.

The dye is added to the textile; it is not present naturally.
The dye cannot be added haphazardly. Instructions as to correct quantities and method must be followed to achieve good results.
Even if the correct instructions are followed, not *all* the dye adheres to the fabric.

(The pupils may have carried out this experiment in *The Basic Course*, Chapter 20.)

Q 7

Communicating
(speech and
writing)

Not all the dye will adhere to the fabric, so dyeing may not be an easy process to carry out every time.

Q 8
With cotton, the dye is taken up readily and a definite colour will result on the fabric.

Q 9 and Q 10
The polyester should be much paler than the cotton. Any dye that is taken up will easily be washed out in hot water.
Anything that remains will be in sharp contrast to the cotton, where a little may come out on washing but a definite strong colour will still be present.

Reasoning
logically

The dye which worked on cotton did not work on polyester, so the answer to question 11 is no. The chemical compositions of cotton and polyester are different. It should be expected that the dye, which is a chemical, would react differently with them.

Observing

Conclusions can now be drawn about the nature of dyes and their relationship to fibres. Pupils should be reminded that dyestuffs are just chemicals and that fibres are also chemicals. Some form of combination took place between the cotton and the dyestuff. That is, the molecules of cotton (mainly cellulose — see Chapter 5) and the molecules of the dyestuff joined together in some way. Very little, if any, reaction took place between the molecules of polyester and the dyestuff molecules.

Applying
knowledge

The conclusion is therefore obvious that a different dyestuff may be needed for polyester than for cotton and this is true for all the fibres. Dyestuffs are generally thought of in classes, a

Observing

class of dyestuff being particularly suitable for one or two fibres but not for others. Some of the names of classes of dyestuffs may be familiar. *Vat* dyes and *direct* dyes are classes suitable for cotton. For polyester the class of dye generally used is called a *disperse* dye.

Worksheets FM10, FM11, and FM12 are about the colour fastness of household dyes to light, washing, and dry cleaning, and the effectiveness of different types of commercial dyes.

Extension work

Using
references

The information regarding the history of dyestuffs, that is the original vegetable and animal sources used, may be followed up. The pupils may make up their own dyes and experiment with

Practical
skills

dyeing suitable fabric samples.

Dyes may be made up using onion skins, blackberries, and various other kinds of vegetable matter. Many books are available on this art. Samples of fabrics can then be dyed and compared for the take-up and fastness of the dye.

The industry changed radically with the discovery of the first synthetic dyestuff. Instead of having to rely on chemicals from plant and animal sources, substances were made synthetically, that is, built up from simple chemicals. Today these are usually derived from oil; originally they were produced from coal.

10.3
FINGERPRINTS

Main ideas in this section

Dyes absorb colours in varying proportions.

This is how shades and tints are made.

Identifying causes	Having established the simple principle of colour production by subtraction from white light by dyestuffs, it is natural to develop this into an understanding of how the vast range of shades and hues of colours are achieved. To do this requires the concept of an additional dimension to the absorption of colours by dyestuffs. So far it has been thought of as an all or nothing process. Red has meant everything absorbed from white light except red which is totally reflected. In practice this never happens. The dyestuff absorbs a percentage of each of the colours, but the percentage absorbed varies. Thus it might absorb 50 per cent red, 30 per cent orange, 10 per cent yellow, 80 per cent blue, 70 per cent green, 40 per cent indigo and 40 per cent violet. The resulting mixture reflected will therefore be 50 per cent red, 70 per cent orange, 90 per cent yellow, 20 per cent blue, 30 per cent green, 60 per cent indigo and 60 per cent violet.
Communicating (graphs) Assessing (relevant factors)	One way of representing this idea is as a graph. The horizontal axis represents the wavelength and hence a particular colour. The vertical axis shows the percentage absorbed at each wavelength or colour. Every dyestuff has its own individual absorption spectrum graph which is a kind of fingerprint for that dyestuff.

Q 13
Figure 10.3 shows the absorption spectrum of a dyestuff giving an orange—red colour.

Interpreting (graphs)	*Q 14* Now introduce the idea of combining dyestuffs to give a wider range of colours. Remind the pupils that for two or more dyes to be used on the same fabric, they must both be of the right class of dyestuff for the fabric being coloured. The colour obtained by using two or more dyestuffs is simply what is left when the absorption spectra of the dyes are combined.

Worksheet FM13 introduces pupils to the idea of tints and explains how they can be achieved with commercial dyes.

Observing	*Q 15* The absorption spectra of the dyes in *figures 10.3* and *10.4* combined indicate that virtually all the range of wavelength is absorbed by one dye or another in the mixture. The result will therefore be black as no light will be reflected. In dyeing textiles the colour black is often obtained by mixing dyestuffs.

Interpreting (graphs)	*Ideas for homework* Pupils could be given graphs representing different colours and asked to identify them.

Concepts and skills	Pupils may be able to:
10.1 *Subtraction* Colour spectrum. Subtraction of colour.	State the colour components of visible light.
Science/maths Light. Electromagnetic spectrum.	Explain that colour is caused by substances in the fabric absorbing some colours and reflecting the rest.
Applying knowledge, Communicating (speech and writing), Reasoning logically.	Explain what the result will be if all the colours are absorbed and no light is reflected, or *vice versa*.
10.2 *Dyes* Dyes. Pigments. Bonding.	State that a dyestuff is a pigment which can bond to a fibre and remain fast.
Science/maths Dyes. Pigments.	Recognize that fast dyes remain bonded to the fabric.
Observing, Applying knowledge, Communicating (speech and writing), Reasoning logically.	Explain that dyes and fibres are chemicals with different affinities, therefore different classes of dyes will be needed for different fibres.
10.3 *Fingerprints* Absorption spectra of dyes. Shades and tints.	Identify the colours on absorption spectrum graphs.
Science/maths Electromagnetic spectrum. Graphs.	Recall that the percentages of colour absorbed and reflected produce the variety of shades.
Observing, Interpreting (graphs), Communicating (speech and writing), Assessing (relevant factors), Using references, Classifying.	By investigation find out what types of dyes are available for home dyeing and what fibres they are suitable for.

Using
references

Classifying

They could find out what types of dyes are available for home dyeing and what fibres they are suitable for. Alternatively they could find out what colour dyes come from various animal and vegetable sources.

This chapter's Background reading encourages pupils to think about the use of colour for different purposes and its effects. You could discuss the different ways in which the room shown in *figure 10.5* could be furnished. Some pupils might like to produce their own designs and colour-schemes for different rooms.

CHAPTER 11

Putting colour into practice

The previous chapter investigated the theory behind colour and its application to textiles. Now the commercial application of colour in both dyeing and printing techniques is considered. Pupils learn that different aesthetic effects are produced by varying the point in the chain at which dyeing occurs. They also look at various printing techniques, including the recently developed transfer printing methods.

Time allocation
Sections 11.1 and 11.2: 80 minutes; sections 11.3, 11.4, and 11.5: 80 minutes.

Extension work in this chapter
Section 11.4: practical screen printing to demonstrate the process.
Section 11.5: investigating and comparing paper printing and fabric printing techniques.

Worksheet and Assessment card Master
FM29   Assessment card

11.1
COMMERCIAL PRACTICE

Main ideas in this section

For successful dyeing, the dye and fibre must be carefully matched and the conditions carefully controlled.

The dye is usually dissolved or suspended in water.

In industry many factors must be considered by the dyer. First the correct colour must be achieved and this often means matching colours from another fabric. If the colour to be matched is on a different fibre, the same dyestuff probably cannot be used (see section 10.3). Whatever dyestuff or combination of dyestuffs is used to provide the correct colour match, it will have to be fast to the new fibre. If fibre blends are being used the problem may be compounded; a different class of dye must be selected for each fibre and yet the same colour must be produced on each. The dyer must also select dyestuffs which may be applied to the fibre without damaging it. The dye must be taken up evenly, and finally the dyer must attempt to achieve this at a reasonable cost. In other words the dyer must consider the three factors — aesthetics, performance, and price.

Dye is usually applied from a solution or suspension in water. A suspension means that the dye is dispersed as very fine particles in water rather than being totally dissolved in it. Commercial dyeing machines simply carry out what was done by hand in section 10.3, but they have facilities for increasing the temperature to boiling-point (100 °C) and sometimes above by using pressure vessels. The dyeing machines vary depending on what stage the colour is added.

The idea that colour can be added at various points in the process can now be introduced. The dye can be added to the fibre, the yarn, or the fabric. For man-made fibres it can be added at the polymer stage too. *Figure 11.2* shows dyeing machines.

Applying knowledge

Identifying causes

Most pupils will be familiar with printing as a method of applying colour to fabrics. It has certain basic differences from dyeing. When dyeing is carried out, whether in fibre, yarn, or fabric form, the whole item is immersed in the dye. If the correct dye is applied under the correct conditions it will penetrate the whole textile evenly. It will appear the same from all angles and on both sides of the fabric. In printing the design is applied to one side. Although it penetrates into the fabric, it is never so clear on the back and sometimes not even visible. (*Figure 11.1* shows this.)

Discuss the advantages of printing. Very complicated patterns can be achieved which would be very difficult if not impossible to produce by weaving or knitting. However, the colour still relies on the same principle, and the dyes used are essentially the same.

11.2
ALL THOSE PATTERNS

Main ideas in this section

Textiles can be dyed at the fibre, yarn, or fabric stage.

Different patterns can be produced by the various methods.

This section shows how pattern and colour variety is built up in woven and knitted fabrics. Start from the simple concept of dyeing the whole fabric, and then remind the pupils of the chain of processes (Chapter 2). It is conventional to put dyeing and finishing (Chapter 12) as the next stage after weaving or knitting, but clearly this need not be so.

Q 1
The colour can be added to the polymer itself (before spinning in the case of man-made fibres), the fibre, the yarn, or the fabric.

Clearly if machinery and dyestuffs are available to dye fabric, then suitable machinery could be devised and the same dyestuffs used to dye either the fibre or the yarn. If pupils ask why the garments are not generally dyed, the answer is that in some cases they are. Knitwear is usually produced almost in complete garment form before it is dyed, but of course knitwear has very few trimmings, probably only a sewing thread. A garment such as a jacket or trousers has a lot of trimmings. Dyeing usually means immersing in water. This would mean the fabric and all the trimmings would be dyed. Therefore the trimmings would be affected in some way. It would never be possible to press the garment back to exactly the same shape, and in any event pressing costs money. This is why, commercially, garment dyeing is reserved for simple garments such as knitwear. With synthetic fibres the dye can be introduced to the molten polymer (this is called a *melt* or *polymer dye*). However, this is not often done because it is only economic when large quantities of the same colour are required. It costs too much to change colours frequently to keep pace with fashion. Fibre dyeing is common and results in mixture yarns, although sometimes fibres of all one colour are spun into yarn, and then woven or knitted to give a plain colour fabric. This is more expensive than piece dyeing the fabric, but it gives a better handle. Here is another example of the aesthetics, performance, and price equation. *Figure 11.3* shows one result of mixture fibres.

Q 2

This is best answered by some form of coloured drawing. The important point is to recognize that the woven check pattern is built up by taking different coloured yarns in both warp and weft.

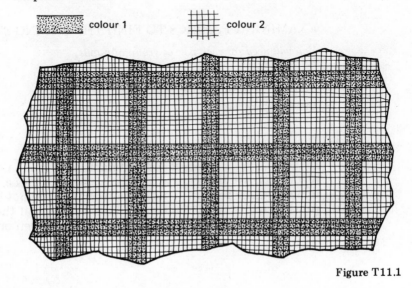

Figure T11.1

For a striped fabric different colours could be used in either warp or weft (normally the warp) and a single colour in the other direction.

Observing
The next stage in using dyed yarns is to employ complex mechanisms for selecting different coloured yarns on a loom or jersey machine to give patterned effects. *Figure 11.4* shows a fairly simple pattern — a check. *Figure 11.5* shows a more complex pattern resulting from coloured yarn selection by Jacquard.

Q 3

Identifying causes
If the fabric were made of two different fibres which took up dyestuff differently, a patterned effect would be produced.

The actual pattern depends on how the fibres are mixed. If staple fibres are mixed in the yarn and then these yarns made up into fabrics, the result would be a mixture or tweedy effect. If yarns are made from a single fibre and then different yarns from different fibres are mixed, the result could be checks, stripes, or complex Jacquard patterns.

The technique is known as *cross dyeing*. Sometimes a single dyestuff is used so one fibre is dyed and the other remains white, or two dyestuffs are used, one giving colour to one fibre and the second giving a different colour to the second fibre. The pupils may have learned about this in *The Basic Course*, Chapter 20.

Reasoning logically
In piece dyeing a fabric made from two fibres (*e.g.* polyester and cotton or polyester and viscose) where only one colour is required, several different dyestuffs may have to be used to achieve this.

EXAMINING FABRICS TO FIND THE DYEING STAGES

You will need for each pair or group of pupils
Fabric samples
(*e.g.* tweeds, fabrics containing complex yarns such as bouclé, stripes, checks, and Jacquards)

Dissecting needle
Hand lens

Q 4

Observing

Suggesting hypotheses
If the exercise is approached systematically, it should not be difficult to see the stage at which dyeing took place. Piece dyeing will be readily apparent, although it will not be possible with the equipment available to decide if the sample has been fibre-dyed in one colour and then woven or knitted.

116

In fibre and yarn dye look out for complex designs where two single-ply yarns of different colours are twisted together to give a complex yarn, one single-ply yarn being fibre-dyed and the other yarn-dyed. If the yarns are not examined carefully they may be mistaken for a single mixture yarn.

Q 5

At first sight it may not appear obvious which is the cheapest method and which the most expensive. Generally, fabric dyeing is the cheapest. It results in one colour and can be done in a continuous process. Fibre dyeing is the next cheapest. Large quantities of fibres can be processed at one time and handled fairly easily. If, however, mixture yarns are produced the blending of different colours can add to the cost. Yarn dyeing is the most expensive, as the yarn must be handled very carefully. It is wound onto special packages for dyeing and then rewound for use in weaving or knitting.

11.3
ROLLERS: CHEAP AND SIMPLE

Main ideas in this section

Fabric printing can be done using blocks or rollers.

Roller printing is relatively quick and cheap.

Most pupils will have carried out some form of block printing at some stage in their school career. Remind them that this type of printing takes a long time, and that in particular it is difficult to line up the blocks so the pattern is repeated accurately.
For some types of garments, a crude hand block effect is desired to create a particular aesthetic effect.

Figure 11.6
This photograph reminds the pupils of a type of printing they may have done in primary school.

Q 6
This refers to the handling difficulties in block printing.

The next concept is important. This is the change from an intermittent process (hand block) to a continuous process (a roller). The design is raised on the surface in both cases but one is slow whereas the other is fast. Where one is difficult to line up the other can be fairly easily controlled. The problem remains, however, that a different roller is required for each
colour. *Figure 11.7* shows roller printing.

An important aesthetic consideration is that the fineness of detail often required cannot be achieved by this method. Relate

<table>
<tr><td>Assessing
(relevant
factors)</td><td>this again to aesthetics, performance, and price. In commercial practice the initial cost of a roller (and remember one roller per colour is needed) is high. However, the rollers can be used almost indefinitely. There are rollers in use today which were produced fifty years ago. Therefore, provided a large quantity of one print is required, the cost is relatively low.</td></tr>
</table>

11.4
SCREENS: EXPENSIVE AND COMPLICATED

Main ideas in this section

Screen printing is an alternative method of printing fabric.

A screen works like a stencil.

Figure 11.8
This shows a simple screen with a design set up.

Discuss the similarity between hand block printing and screens for speed and accuracy of printing. The difference is that fine detail can be obtained with screens.

<table>
<tr><td>Applying
knowledge

Communicating
(speech)</td><td>*Q 7*
The question asks how screen printing could be automated to speed the process. You should get the reply 'make a cylindrical screen, *i.e.*, a screen like a roller'. This has in practice been achieved. The first rotary screens have been available since the 1960s, but before that the flat screen printing had also been automated.</td></tr>
<tr><td>Assessing
(relevant
factors)

Reasoning
logically</td><td>As with rollers, one screen is needed for each colour. They are cheaper to produce than rollers, but they do not last as long. For short runs, screens will be cheaper and give more detail. For long runs the rollers become progressively cheaper, although still unable to give the fineness of detail. Commercially, printing by rotary screen is the most popular as it fits in with the modern requirements of fashion. There are, however, many areas where long runs are still required, such as curtaining materials and pyjama fabrics, and so rollers are still used.</td></tr>
<tr><td>Practical
skills</td><td>*Extension work*
If printing screens are available either in the needlecraft or art rooms, experiments can be carried out which can help to demonstrate the processes involved.</td></tr>
</table>

11.5
ANOTHER WAY

Main ideas in this section

Transfer printing is a relatively new method of printing fabric.

The dyes are first put on paper and then transferred to the fabric.

The method of printing now to be discussed is the most important advance in textile colouring for many years. It has been
predicted that it will be the most important printing process
for textiles by 1990 and may also be used for a large number
of plain coloured fabrics. It works in a different way from
conventional dyeing and printing. Instead of using water-based
dyestuff, the print is transferred by dry heat from previously
printed paper to the fabric. Paper is easily and relatively cheaply
printed. The paper is printed with special dyestuffs which will
transfer on heating to the fabric. The overall cost may not be
very great although two processes are involved, that is, printing
the paper and printing the fabric. Printing the paper requires
the production of rollers — one per colour — but the printing
of paper takes place at a much higher rate than fabric printing
by rollers. The paper printing method usually used is *gravure*
or *flexographic*.

Communicating (speech)   Transfer printing can be done as shown in *figure 11.9* for
complete rolls of paper to complete rolls of fabric. It can also
be used to transfer simple motifs directly onto garments such
as T-shirts. The motifs using disperse dyes for polyester should
not be confused with other types of motifs used for fibres such
as cotton. These do not use dyestuffs as such, but use a plastic
which softens under heat and is pressed into the fibre where it
adheres.

Assessing (relevant factors)   The importance of transfer printing lies in its relative cheapness,
and in that it is a dry process and so can be used in factories
where the services needed for liquid waste disposal and conventional printing are not available. In addition, the level of fastness is extremely high.

The first transfer prints were developed in France and given
the name 'Sublistatic'. This was derived from 'subli' meaning
by sublimation and 'static' from the idea of fastness.

Extension work
Pupils could investigate the techniques of paper printing to
compare with those employed for fabric printing.

Concepts and skills	Pupils may be able to:
11.1 *Commercial practice* Dyeing processes. Aesthetic, performance, and price factors. *Science/maths* Dye technology. Solutions. Suspensions. Applying knowledge, Communicating (writing), Identifying causes.	List the technical factors the dyer must consider, *e.g.* correct colour, dye to fibre, dye fastness, safe method, cost. Explain the difference between printing and dyeing. Describe solutions and suspensions as they apply to dyes.
11.2 *All those patterns* Stages of dyeing: polymer, fibre, yarn, fabric. *Science/maths* Dye technology. Observing, Applying knowledge, Communicating (writing and speech).	Identify given examples of polymer, fibre, yarn, and fabric dyeing. Explain how dyeing at different stages gives different pattern and colour effects. Describe some of the economic factors involved, *e.g.* quality and fashion demand.
11.3 *Rollers: cheap and simple* Printing techniques: blocks and rollers. *Science/maths* Technology of textile printing. Applying knowledge, Communicating (writing and speech), Reasoning logically, Evaluating.	Describe block and roller printing. Explain why roller printing may be more economical than block printing. Describe the main difference between screen printing and block printing in relation to the quality of the finished design.
11.4 *Screens: expensive and complicated* Screen printing. *Science/maths* Textile technology; screen printing. Applying knowledge, Communicating (writing).	Descibe how screen printing is carried out. Discuss the issues of speed and accuracy for fine detail.

Concepts and skills	Pupils may be able to:
11.5 *Another way* Transfer printing. *Science/maths* Sublimation. Applying knowledge, Communicating (writing and speech), Practical skills.	Describe the transfer printing method. Discuss how the print is transferred by contact with a hot dry surface from paper to fabric, and how this differs from motifs which use a plastic which softens under heat and is pressed into the fabric where it adheres. Use a prepared piece of transfer printed material for an article for use in the home.

TRANSFER PRINTING

You will need for each pair or group of pupils
Transfer printing paper
Polyester fabric
15-ml (table) spoon washing powder
Clock or watch with seconds hand
Iron pre-heated to its highest setting
Ironing board
Washing-up bowl

Practical
skills

Applying
knowledge

Observing

The usual temperature for transferring these prints is 180 °C to 200 °C, applied for about 15 seconds. Test that the iron is approximately the right heat by carrying out a dummy experiment, using blank paper and the polyester fabric. If the polyester shows signs of melting, the iron is too hot. Reduce the temperature. This test is to allow for any irregularity in the thermostat of the iron. Make sure, as far as possible, that the pressing is even over the whole print. If the iron is moved the print will be blurred. After printing, the fabric can be tested for fastness of the dye.

Some schools may have purchased a small bench transfer printing press. If this is available it should of course be used instead, according to the manufacturer's instructions.

Q 8
The dye should be fast to hand-hot water and detergent. It may even withstand boiling, although if this is done the fabric may become very creased.

Q 9
The answer should be yes. If not, ask the pupils why they think this is so. It could be that the iron moved, the paper moved, or even that the iron was not hot enough.

Transfer printing uses disperse dyes. These work mainly on polyester. The early transfer prints were not fast to other fibres except sometimes acetate. New developments are increasing the range of fibres which can be printed by this method, but it still works best on polyester.

Ideas for homework

Observing   Pupils could collect (or be given) samples of dyed and printed fabrics and be told to distinguish between them. They could
Classifying   also try to identify the stage at which dyeing took place.

The Background reading tells pupils about the work of one fabric designer. It gives them an idea of how the printed fabrics they buy, wear, and see around them have been created. You could remind pupils of the piece on the buyer in Chapter 1: the designer must produce something that customers will choose to buy.

CHAPTER 12

It's all in the finish

After a fibre has been produced and coloured by whatever combination of processes, a number of additional processes may still be carried out before it is ready to progress along the chain to the garment trade. These processes are termed *finishing*, and may involve physical and chemical methods, which can alter performance properties greatly.

Time allocation
Section 12.1, 12.2, and 12.3: 40 minutes; 12.4 and 12.5: two lessons of 40 minutes each; 12.6: 40 minutes; 12.7: 40 minutes.

Extension work in this chapter
Section 12.7: examining garments to find out how waterproof they are.

Worksheet and Assessment card Masters
FM14 Minimum-iron finish
FM15 Superwash wool
FM16 Water repellency
FM30 Assessment card

12.1
GREY FABRIC

Main ideas in this section

Finishing is a very important part of the manufacture of textiles.

It may completely change the aesthetics or performance of a fabric.

Applying knowledge

Finishing may add considerably to the cost of the product. An example is the finishing carried out on fine worsted suitings; ten separate processes can easily be involved. In this book only a few finishes are considered. The three main ones chosen are those which have a significant effect on performance properties. There are various ways of classifying finishes in textile technology books. None of these classifications mean much in the trade itself. As a simple guide they can be divided into physical and chemical techniques. Physical methods generally relate to aesthetics, and chemical methods to performance; hence chemical techniques are often referred to as *functional* finishes. Some

Classifying

finishes are referred to as 'routine' as they are carried out on practically everything and are usually physical.

The term for a fabric before finishing is 'grey' or 'greige'. The way it is spelled is historical in certain sections of the trade. It does not refer to its colour, rather that it is probably dirty.

12.2
CLEANING IT UP

Main idea in this section

Physical finishes include cleaning and 'stentering'.

Identifying causes

All fabric is cleaned because inevitably it becomes dirty during manufacture, often from oil from machinery. A great deal of jersey fabric is dry cleaned but most other fabrics are scoured, *i.e.* washed. The type of bleach used prior to scouring depends on the fibre. For instance, wool is very sensitive.

Q 1 and Q 2

Communicating (speech)

Domestic bleach produces chlorine. This has a severe bleaching action very harmful to wool. If it is concentrated it may be corrosive to the skin. Bleach should be kept out of the reach of children and never transferred from its original ⚠ bottle.

The process of stentering is not only concerned with drying but also stabilizing many fabrics, particularly synthetics. Certain fabrics require additional physical finishing to stabilize them, including compressive shrinkage treatments (sometimes called by the trade names Sanforized or Rigmel) for cotton fabrics.

12.3
AESTHETIC CHANGES

Main ideas in this section

There are numerous physical finishes concerned with appearance.

Examples are calendering and brushing.

Other processes used in different trades include crabbing (wool), decatizing (wool, silk, viscose), fulling (wool), shearing (wool and man-made fibre), singeing (man-made fibres, particularly polyester), moiré (silk and man-made fibre), and schreinering (nylon and polyester and cotton).

Applying knowledge	Sometimes physical processing can affect performance properties quite markedly. Various brushing techniques which raise the surface obviously increase the thickness.
Reasoning logically	*Q 3* Increasing thickness will increase the insulation and so keep the wearer warmer.
Communicating (speech)	If the brushing damages fibres it can decrease the strength. Other surface raising techniques are called gigging and napping.

EXAMINING WARP-KNIT NYLON AND WARP-KNIT BRUSHED NYLON

You will need for each pair or group of pupils
Sample of warp-knit nylon
Sample of warp-knit brushed nylon
Hand lens

Practical skills	Preferably use samples of the same fabric in its flat and brushed form. This activity can be undertaken fairly quickly as pupils should by now be familiar with the techniques of assessing handle.
	Q 4 The brushed nylon.
Estimating Measuring	Point out how easily the surface can be compressed and so how difficult it is to measure the thickness.
Observing Identifying causes	*Q 5* Warp-knit nylon is made from multi-filament yarn. If the brushing is carried out correctly it raises small loops of individual filaments to form the brushed surface. These can be observed with a hand lens. These loops will hook onto small rough patches on the skin, particularly at the corner of nails, which can give an unpleasant sensation.

12.4
PERFORMANCE CHANGES

Main ideas in this section

Chemical finishes can cause great changes in performance.

Resin-treated cotton dries quickly and needs little ironing.

Communicating (speech)	*Q 6* Chemical finishes will have a more dramatic effect. They can break the fibre molecule or change it in some way so that in a sense it is not the same chemical compound.

125

IS IT STILL COTTON?

Assessing
(relevant
factors)
Some of the chemicals applied are believed to link onto the cotton molecule so that arguably it is no longer cotton. Certainly the performance is greatly changed. The treatment is usually termed *resin* treatment, but resin is simply another name for polymer. What occurs is that the cotton fabric is passed through a mixture of two chemicals. The chemicals combine together to give a polymer and the polymer is dispersed, rather like a lattice, throughout the cotton.

The original discoveries were made at the laboratories of the Tootal Company and, at first, were thought of as a means of stabilizing cotton fabric. It was only some years later that the value of improved wrinkle recovery and quick drying were realized. *Figure 12.3* shows a typical advertisement.

Virtually all cotton fabrics are now treated in this way, largely as a way of competing with synthetic fabrics. Viscose is also treated like this because it is a cellulosic fibre.

Q 7

Assessing
(relevant
factors)

Communicating
(speech)
Towels would not be resin-treated. Quick drying implies hydrophobic properties which would be a disadvantage in a towel. Here is another example of properties required being incompatible in textiles. Likewise T-shirts are not resin-treated because they would not absorb perspiration if they were.

COMPARING THE WASHING PERFORMANCE OF PURE COTTON AND RESIN-TREATED COTTON

You will need for each pair or group of pupils
Pure cotton fabric, 15-cm square
Resin-treated cotton fabric, 15-cm square
Detergent

Access to washing machine

Observing

Organizing
and analysing
data
The samples may need to be sewn around the edges to prevent fraying. There is no need to use excessive detergent. It is best to remove the samples from the machine before spinning, so that the speed of drying can be fully compared.

Q 8

Communicating
(graphs)
The improved wrinkle recovery and quick drying of the resin-treated cotton should be apparent.

12.5
CHANGES ARE NOT ALWAYS GOOD!

Main idea in this section

Resin-treated cotton is not as durable as untreated cotton, and is not as comfortable to wear.

Identifying causes

Although improvements have been made in the resins over the years, so that at their best cotton fabrics can be boiled and after drying require very little ironing, little advance has been made in reducing the loss of durability. The probable reason is the chemical combination of the resin with the cellulose molecules, breaking the length of the polymer and thus reducing its strength. This problem has bedevilled the resin treatment of cotton.

Assessing (relevant factors)

This loss of strength is probably the main reason why polyester/cotton fabrics, although not giving quite such a good minimum-iron performance, have gained in popularity over resin-treated 100 per cent cotton. Where resin-treated cotton is used it is likely to be heavy in weight in an attempt to balance the loss of strength.

Reasoning logically

Another factor, not always appreciated, is that the loss of hydrophilic properties reduces the comfort claim of cotton. Stress this point, because cotton goods are still sold on this image even though they are often resin-treated.

COMPARING THE DURABILITY OF PURE COTTON AND RESIN-TREATED COTTON

You will need for each pair or group of pupils
Sample of pure cotton
Sample of resin-treated cotton

Scissors
Weights
Hook
Spring balance

Practical skills

Measuring

It is important to use the same fabric treated and untreated. Commercially, durability is difficult to measure in the laboratory. This test simulates the Elmendorf Tear Strength Tester which is generally used for resin-treated cotton. It is probably easier to carry out the test with a spring balance (see figure T3.1).

Q 9

Organizing and analysing data

Pure cotton is more durable.

Worksheet FM14 shows pupils how to treat fabric with a resin and asks them to test its effects.

12.6
WHAT ABOUT WOOL?

Main idea in this section

Wool shrinkage can be prevented by chemical treatment.

The success of acrylic has been due mainly to its washing performance against wool and its lower price. This has been particularly important for children's wear. If a successful machine washable process had been available for wool in the early 1960s it is possible that acrylic would never have been successful.

PUTTING IT RIGHT

The development of this process began with work in the research laboratories of the International Wool Secretariat (I.W.S.). The process is another example of rebalancing the aesthetic, performance, and price factors. The full process involves:

1 chemical treatment to open positions on the wool molecule so that a nylon polymer can be attached
2 adding the nylon polymer
3 attaching a softening agent to the end of the nylon polymer.

As all these chemicals are joined to each other and to the wool by chemical bonds, the treatment is durable. *Figure 12.6* shows the difference the treatment makes.

Worksheet FM15 describes an experiment which demonstrates how treated woollen material behaves when it is washed.

12.7
KEEPING OUT THE RAIN

Main ideas in this section

Waterproof clothes have obvious uses but are uncomfortable to wear because perspiration cannot pass through them.

A compromise is to treat fabric with silicone so that it is fairly waterproof and fairly comfortable.

This is a brief consideration of the problems of water proofing and the need to compromise.

Everyone is familiar with rubber macintoshes and plastic raincoats, and how even with air holes under the arm they become wet inside due to perspiration. This remains the only way to obtain a completely waterproof garment.

Concepts and skills	Pupils may be able to:
12.1 *Grey fabric* Fabric finishing. *Science/maths* Textile technology. Chemical and physical techniques of fabric finishing. Applying knowledge, Communicating (writing and speech), Observing, Using references.	Name the term for a fabric before finishing. Explain that finishes are used to improve aesthetic or performance properties. List the finishes commonly used on household fabrics.
12.2 *Cleaning it up* Physical finishes: cleaning and stentering. *Science/maths* Properties of materials: compression, shrinkage, physical change. Applying knowledge, Using references, Communicating (writing), Deciding criteria, Identifying causes.	Suggest how fabrics become dirty during manufacture, *e.g.* from contact with machinery and handling. Explain cleaning methods such as dry cleaning or washing, and explain why bleaching can be harmful. Explain that stentering dries and stabilizes fabrics. Name and describe other physical finishes, *e.g.* pressing, teasing.
12.3 *Aesthetic changes* Calendering and brushing. *Science/maths* Physical change. Estimating, Measuring, Observing, Using references, Deciding criteria, Suggesting hypotheses, Designing tests, Reasoning logically.	Distinguish between brushed and calendered finishes correctly. Relate these finishes to aesthetic factors. Discuss limitations when fabrics are in use, such as resistance to soiling and wear.

Concepts and skills	Pupils may be able to:
12.4 *Performance changes* and **12.5** *Changes are not always good!* Chemical changes: resin treatments; advantages and disadvantages. *Science/maths* Chemical compounds. Chemical change. Polymers. Applying knowledge, Communicating (writing), Assessing (relevant factors), Organizing data.	Say which fabric is often resin-treated. Describe how resin treatment improves wrinkle recovery and speed of drying, but creates hydrophobic properties. State the main disadvantages of resin treatment and give examples of inappropriate use.
12.6 *What about wool?* and **12.7** *Keeping out the rain* Fabric finishes. Balancing aesthetic, performance, and price factors. *Science/maths* Chemical change. Properties of materials. Using references, Applying knowledge, Communicating (writing), Classifying, Deciding criteria, Identifying causes.	Describe the method of preventing shrinkage in wool. Explain and describe how this is brought about by chemical changes. Discuss the problems involved in putting a waterproof finish on a fabric.

IS A COMPROMISE POSSIBLE?

Silicones are types of polymer based on the elements silicon and oxygen. Types of silicones are familiar from their addition to polishes and uses in lubricants. The type of silicone used on so-called 'raincoats' is reasonably 'durable' to washing but is removed by dry cleaning. Silicones are applied in a finishing works so the 'reproofing' or 'retexturizing' done by dry cleaners will not use silicones. The silicone works by increasing the surface tension. This makes it more likely that the water will remain as a drop and run off.

Reasoning
logically

Identifying
causes

Designing tests

Extension work

The pupils could examine a raincoat, anorak, and kagoul and try to find out how waterproof they are by putting drops of water on them.

Worksheet FM16 shows pupils how to use Zepel or Scotchgard on a variety of fabrics and how to test their effectiveness.

Assessing (relevant factors)

Ideas for homework

Pupils could look through their wardrobes or mail order catalogues to identify examples of fabrics which have had the finishing treatments mentioned in the text.

The Background reading is about protective clothing. Encourage pupils to consider the circumstances in which they wear protective clothing and the different factors that have been taken into account when designing it, such as cost and acceptability.

CHAPTER 13

The garment takes shape

Many textile courses seem to assume that nothing of importance happens after the fabric is produced. This is far from correct. It is important that the properties are retained, and if possible enhanced, in the conversion of the two-dimensional fabric to the three-dimensional garment.

This requires care in making up and selecting trimmings. Although this chapter concentrates on garments, the same principles apply to household textiles too.

Time allocation
Sections 13.1 and 13.2: 40 minutes; 13.3: two 40-minute lessons; 13.4: two 40-minute lessons; 13.5 and 13.6: two 40-minute lessons.

Extension work in this chapter
Section 13.2: drafting patterns — designing a simple skirt; additional experiments with pressing away fullness.

Worksheet and Assessment card Master
FM31   Assessment card

13.1
TWO-DIMENSIONAL TO THREE-DIMENSIONAL

Main idea in this section

For clothing, fabrics must be converted from two-dimensional to three-dimensional form.

Reasoning logically

Continue the one-dimensional yarn to two-dimensional fabric to three-dimensional garment story. Pupils are generally familiar with the idea of three dimensions and should readily see the mathematical progression.

13.2
ENGINEERING THE SHAPE

Main ideas in this section

Pieces of fabric with curved edges are joined together to produce three-dimensional shapes.

Three-dimensional shapes can also be produced by moulding as in tailoring.

Suggesting
hypotheses
The word engineering is used deliberately, so that what is being done can be related to engineering processes as a whole. The principles are the same whether a ship or car is being fabricated from sheet metal, or a garment is being made from a 'sheet' of fabric. Clothing is traditionally made by cutting various shapes and joining them together. If two straight edges are joined as in *figure 13.3*, no three-dimensional shape results (*i.e.* it is a flat seam).

Communicating
(speech)
Q 1
If the edges are curved, a three-dimensional shape results. If pupils have difficulty visualizing this you could demonstrate it.

Reasoning
logically
Make sure pupils realize that the designer is not only a stylist but also the person who has to ensure fit. Actually, in the trade, the functions are sometimes separated. A person who has a particular flair for creating style need not necessarily be the person who finally designs the patterns. Many of the famous 'designers' are mainly stylists. But since aesthetics are so important, they are a vital part of the textile chain. The person who creates the pattern rather than the style and reproduces it for various sizes is sometimes called a pattern cutter. *Figure 13.5* shows a style drawing and the shapes of the pieces of cloth needed.

Communicating
(speech)
Q 2
A few examples of fashion designers are: Dior, Chanel, Bill Gibb, Mary Quant, Hardy Amies, Zandra Rhodes, Jean Muir, Yves St Laurent.

Practical
skills

Estimating

Measuring

Communicating
(diagrams)
Extension work
Pupils could design a simple skirt. There are many texts about pattern cutting which give clear instructions on the techniques involved.

You will need for each pair of pupils
Squared paper and/or pattern drafting paper
Pencil
Ruler and metre rule
Tape measure

ANOTHER WAY

Reasoning
logically
Applying
knowledge
Consider moulding firstly in engineering terms as an alternative way of achieving a three-dimensional shape. *Figure 13.4* should help with this. Moulding of this type has to date a limited use in textiles.

Observation
v
inference

Patterns would be distorted.

Moulding could become an increasingly important method for making clothing as it has for footwear. Felt hats are made in this way (*figure 13.6*) and moulding is used for making brassière cups.

THE TAILOR'S WAY

Applying
knowledge

In the bespoke tailoring trade and to an increasingly smaller extent in the ready-to-wear trade, extra shape to fit parts of the body is obtained by moulding. Part of this moulding is similar to the type already discussed; for example, when the area of the back over the shoulder blade is pressed to fit a particularly round-shouldered figure.

Identifying
causes

Reasoning
logically

The other type of moulding is the inclusion of fullness, where the extra fabric on one side of the join is pressed away. This curves the seam and gives extra shape on one side. Tailors call this 'shrinking' but the term is misleading. The fabric does not shrink — it is not dimensionally unstable. The fullness is moulded away and accommodated in other parts of the fabric structure. The ability of a fabric to accept fullness depends primarily on its thickness, which generally equates with weight. Heavier, thicker fabrics can absorb a much greater amount of fullness. Fabrics below 200 grams per square metre can absorb virtually nothing. It is this extra shape obtained from fullness and moulding which is the hallmark of the fit obtained by bespoke tailoring (*figure 13.7*). However, this is an expensive process due to the time taken, and increasingly suits are made entirely by engineering.

HOW IS 'FULLNESS' PUT IN?

Practical
skills
Observation
v
inference

You will need for each pair of pupils

Wool suiting fabric	Scissors
Thread	Needle and pins
Iron	Sewing machine
Pressing cloth	

Communicating
(maths)
Assessing
(relevant
factors)

It is important to choose a fabric sufficiently heavy to accommodate the amount of fullness being included. A minimum of 300 grams per square metre is needed (*i.e.* heavy-weight suiting). If wool is not available then polyester/wool can be used. The amount of fullness included is $^2/_{20} \times 100 = 10$ per cent.

Communicating
(speech)

Q 4

The seam will be curved and not lie flat, therefore showing a three-dimensional shape.

Q 5

Applying
knowledge

Q 5
The two main parts where fullness is included on a jacket are the shoulder seam and the sleeve insertion. The join the pupils have just made would be most useful on the shoulder.

Extension work

Communicating
(maths)

Increase the amount of fullness by 2.5 per cent (*i.e.* add 0.5 cm to the longer piece of fabric) and repeat the experiment. Continue doing this until a point is reached where the fullness will not work away.

13.3
JOINING IT UP

Main ideas in this section

Fabric pieces must be joined together in a way that does not diminish their performance or aesthetic value.

Sewing is necessary for this; sticking is very unsatisfactory.

This section emphasizes how the importance of aesthetics and performance goes right through garment making (and indeed household textiles).

COMPARING JOINS

Applying
knowledge

You will need for each pair of pupils

Pure cotton fabric	Sewing machine
Thread	Scissors
P.V.A. glue	Glue brush

Observation
v
inference

Do not attempt to press open the seams. The glued seam would melt and be extremely messy.

Reasoning
logically

Q 6
Apart from the obvious line of sewing, the sewn seam is open, whereas the edges of the glued seam may be totally stuck together. Even if the glue did not melt this would make pressing open very difficult or impossible.

Communicating
(speech and
writing)

Q 7 and Q 8
The glued sample is stiff and inflexible, and has lost the aesthetic qualities of handle and drape.

Q 9 and Q 10
The stitched seam will have had relatively little effect on handle and drape, and is a better method of joining the pieces of fabric.

13.4
SEAMS AND PURPOSES

Main ideas in this section

The seam must be able to stretch as much as the fabric.

Overlock stitch and zig-zag stitch stretch much more than lock stitch.

Reasoning
logically

On the basis that the making up should preserve and not detract from the performance properties of the fabric, the thread must have a number of properties, some of which are listed in section 13.5.

Q 11

Communicating
(speech)

If the seam could not stretch as much as the fabric, it might break when the fabric stretched and the seam could not.

COMPARING THE STRETCH PROPERTIES OF SEAMS

You will need for each pair or group of pupils
6 pieces of double jersey fabric (each 10 cm × 5 cm)
Cotton thread

Ruler
Sewing machine

Practical
skills

Measuring

Sew the seams along the line of the greatest stretch. It is important that the same stitch length (*i.e.* stitches per centimetre) is used (about 4 or 5 stitches per cm). Decreasing the stitch length will increase the stretch in the seam, as there will obviously be more thread in the seam. If a true overlock stitch is not available, use an overedge stitch. Some help may be needed to ensure that pupils do not over-stretch the seam and break the thread.

Q 12

Communicating
(maths)

Applying
knowledge

The overlock and zig-zag will have a higher percentage stretch than the lock stitch. The amount of stretch in the overlock and zig-zag will, in addition, be dependent on the stitch width. It is advisable to keep the width constant for both stitches.

Q 13

Organizing
data

The main advantage is that when pressed open, a lock stitch seam does not gape so much, unless compared with a very narrow zig-zag.

13.5
GETTING THE RIGHT THREAD

Main ideas in this section

The performance of a thread must match that of the fabric.

The most important properties are strength and size retention.

Stretch may also be important. Polyester thread stretches more than cotton.

Cotton thread is more satisfactory for high-speed industrial machines than 100 per cent polyester.

Applying
knowledge

Classifying

Try to get the pupils to list the performance properties required of the sewing thread to match fabric performance. Apart from strength and size retention which are considered here, other important properties may be flame resistance for certain garments and quick drying when a lot of sewing thread is used. *Figure 13.10* shows the result of thread shrinkage. *Figure 13.11* shows poor durability. These are re-emphasized in *figures 13.12* and *13.13*.

Q 14

Applying
knowledge

This is a reminder that weft-knitted fabrics generally give the greatest stretch (see Chapter 9). This is in preparation for a discussion on the need for stretch in a sewing thread when used for a stretch fabric. This is in addition to the need to be able to absorb the stretch present in the seam itself.

COMPARING THE STRETCH PROPERTIES OF SEAMS USING DIFFERENT THREADS

You will need for each pair or group of pupils
4 pieces of double jersey fabric   Ruler
(each 10 cm × 5 cm)   Sewing machine
Cotton thread
Polyester thread of similar size

Practical
skills

Measuring

Designing
tests

Point out that this is a repeat of the previous investigation but with an important difference which shows how scientific experiments are done. Last time all the variables except the type of seam were kept constant. Now everything is kept constant except the sewing thread. Therefore the previous investigation can give a valid comparison of seam types, and this one, of threads.

Q 15

Organizing
data
Communicating
(maths)

The polyester thread will give the largest stretch. Much of the stretch will come from the seam itself. The difference in stretchability of polyester will be an added bonus. For stretch fabrics a polyester thread should give a longer life.

COTTON WINS THE SECOND ROUND

Although industrial sewing machines can sew at 7000 stitches per minute (at least ten times faster than the average domestic machine) they only reach this speed on fairly long seams. Even so, sewing thread breakdown can become a great problem. Polyester thread by itself will melt and completely block the needle eye with polymer.

Suggesting
hypotheses

Q 16

Applying
knowledge

Even if the speed of sewing is kept down, the problem can arise with thick fabrics, or in seams where several thicknesses of thin fabrics are held together. Needle temperatures of over 300 °C have been measured during sewing. Under these conditions polyester will melt.

Communicating
(speech)

Figures 13.14 and 13.16

These show apparatus for measuring the temperature at the eye of a needle, and a tester developed at Leeds University that can assess the likely difficulty of sewing particular fabrics.

COMPROMISE AGAIN

Applying
knowledge

The sewing threads available for domestic use are generally made from staple fibre. Sylko is, of course, cotton. Drima and Star are 100 per cent polyester staple spun on the cotton system. Gutterman is also 100 per cent polyester, spun on the Schappé system. Trylko is an exception: this is made from polyester filament, but texturized by the air-jet process (see Chapter 8). The loops in the structure carry air which acts as an insulator, but whilst the thread is successful on domestic machines it does not perform well, unlike Drima and Star, on high-speed industrial machines.

13.6
OTHER TRIMMINGS

Main idea in this section

The performance of the other trimmings must match that of the main fabric.

Classifying

It would be useful in this last section to refer once again to the three factors and to discuss the properties pupils should look for in the trimmings, bearing in mind what they have learned about fabric performance.

Applying
knowledge

Q 17

a durability and dimensional stability
b durability, especially to flexing, and dimensional stability
c dimensional stability.

Concepts and skills	Pupils may be able to:
13.1 *Two-dimensional to three-dimensional* and **13.2** *Engineering the shape* Garment construction. *Science/maths* Structures; dimensions. Applying knowledge, Communicating (writing and speech), Reasoning logically, Suggesting hypotheses, Practical skills.	List articles made using the heat-setting process. Explain the ways fabrics can be converted to three dimensions, *e.g.* by cutting patterns, moulding, joining. Discuss cost of processing for individual fit versus mass production.
13.3 *Joining it up* and **13.4** *Seams and purposes* Techniques of construction. Aesthetics. Performance. *Science/maths* Properties of materials. Structures. Dimensions. Applying knowledge, Reasoning logically, Organizing data.	State three important types of stitch: lock stitch, zig-zag, and overlock stitch. Suggest that differences in stretch properties and strength of seams are important. Describe how sewing is a technique which can be varied to match the fabric performance; adhesives alter fabric properties.
13.5 *Getting the right thread* and **13.6** *Other trimmings* Thread performance. *Science/maths* Effect of heat on materials. Friction. Textile technology. Classifying, Applying knowledge, Suggesting hypotheses, Organizing data.	List the performance properties which would be ideally provided by a sewing thread. Give trade names for polyester thread (Drima, Star, Gutterman, Trylko). Discuss aesthetic, performance, and price factors in relation to trimmings, giving examples.

Ideas for homework

Pupils could be asked to design garments for particular purposes.

This chapter's Background reading is about fashion design. The pupils should realize that most clothing design is constrained by the needs of mass producers and chain stores. They should be realistic about job opportunities in this field. Some pupils might look at their local shop windows and consider what type of people might buy the clothes displayed in each one.

CHAPTER 14
Getting dirty

A textile item's performance has to be assessed not only during wear but also during cleaning. This chapter examines why cleaning is necessary and why the need for cleaning constantly recurs. The topic is also covered in *The Basic Course* Chapter 22 and *People and homes* Chapter 5.

Time allocation
Two lessons of 40 minutes each.

Worksheet and Assessment card Masters
FM17   Fabric cling and anti-stat
FM32   Assessment card

14.1
LIVING IN DIRT

Main ideas in this section

Dust is fine particles of anything light enough to float for some time in air currents.

It settles on everything including furniture and clothing.

Q 1

Applying knowledge

Identifying causes

Some dust is burned, but the main remover of dust from the surface is probably rain. After a hot dry spell streets become dusty and cars and other objects become coated in fine particles. When the rain comes the dust is damped down and finally drains away to the sea.

EXAMINING DUST CLINGING TO A FABRIC

You will need for each pair or group of pupils
Sample of fabric which has recently been laundered
Small amount of dust

Hand lens

Practical skills

Observation v inference

Just leaving some fabric in a dusty room for a while will produce enough dust. Otherwise use dust from a vacuum cleaner, but note precautions outlined in section 7.6. It should be possible under a hand lens to see how the unevenly shaped dust (*e.g.* hair) becomes hooked into the surface of the fabric. Here it helps if the fabric has a fairly hairy surface.

14.2
REMOVING THE DUST

Main idea in this section

It would be easy to remove dust from clothing if grease and oil were not present.

Reasoning
logically

This little section is important as it leads to the realization that if dust were the only reason why clothes get dirty we would probably not need to wash them.

Q 2

Communicating
(speech)

In addition to shaking, dust could be removed by brushing (clothes brush), beating (carpet beater), or vacuum cleaning.

Assessing
ideas

Because of grease or oil, clothes cannot be kept clean by these means alone. It is necessary to use the far more complicated methods of washing or dry cleaning.

14.3
GREASE FROM WITHIN AND WITHOUT

Main idea in this section

Grease comes from the skin as well as external sources.

Applying
knowledge

Oil or grease from the skin is a continual source of soiling. This should not be confused with the occasional very disastrous soiling which occurs, for example, when painting, work-ing on a car, or digging the garden. *Figure 14.3* illustrates gross soiling.

Reasoning
logically

14.4
HOW DIRTY CAN YOU GET?

Main ideas in this section

Variations in the degree of soiling can be due to human factors or fabric factors.

There are also apparent variations due to the colour of the fabric.

Q 3

Communicating
(speech)

A rough surface is likely to trap more dirt than a smooth surface. This is a variation due to fabric.

Q 4

The surface of a duster is brushed so that it will collect dust easily.

Concepts and skills	Pupils may be able to:
14.1 *Living in dirt* Sources of dust. *Science/maths* Airborne particles. Static. Applying knowledge, Communicating (writing and speech), Observing, Reasoning logically, Identifying causes.	State that dust is fine particles of matter. Explain that soiling is caused by it settling and becoming entangled, and by static attraction. Explain how fabrics vary in the way they attract dust, for reasons such as surface finish, fibre type, and hydrophobic properties.
14.2 *Removing the dust* Physical removal of dust. *Science/maths* Particles, properties of matter. Applying knowledge, Communicating (speech and writing), Practical skills.	State that dust can be removed by brushing, beating, or vacuum cleaning. Realize that other methods become necessary because grease or oil mixed with dust is not removed by physical methods alone. Describe the dry cleaning method and suggest fibres which may require this treatment.
14.3 *Grease from within and without* and **14.4** *How dirty can you get?* Grease stains. *Science/maths* Soiling. Applying knowledge, Communicating (speech and writing), Reasoning logically, Assessing (relevant factors).	State that the most frequent cause of soiling is oil or grease from the skin. Explain that some parts of garments get dirtier than others because some parts of the body are more greasy than others. Explain that stains are caused by accidents, contact with food or with equipment, etc. Discuss why variations in soiling occur. Suggest actions which could be taken to minimize these effects.

Applying
knowledge

Q 5

Static electricity affects fabrics made from hydrophobic fibres: mainly synthetics and resin-treated cotton. This is another variation due to fabric.

The pupils may have used worksheet FM17 to investigate static electricity in Chapter 7. Alternatively they could do so here.

Q 6

Lighter coloured and plain fabrics will appear more dirty than those fabrics whose colour is similar to that of the dirt itself. This is only an apparent variation.

Ideas for homework

The pupils probably take soaps and detergents for granted. The Background reading for this chapter tells them what life was like without them. Some pupils could do projects on the development of soaps and detergents.

CHAPTER 15
Keep it clean

The two methods of removing dirt from clothes and household textiles are dry cleaning and washing. With the advent of synthetic fibres, washing has become even more important. The efficiency of washing depends on the type of detergent used, the water itself, and the washing equipment. The conditions which can be used depend on the fabric and its performance properties. To obtain the best results, washing conditions for different fabrics have been worked out, notably those put forward by the Home Laundering Consultative Council (H.L.C.C.). Examination of this completes the chain of processes.

Time allocation
Section 15.1, 15.2, and 15.3: 80 minutes; 15.4 and 15.5: 160 minutes; 15.6, 15.7, and 15.8: 80 minutes.

Extension work in this chapter
Section 15.5: getting pure water from salty water.

Worksheet and Assessment card Masters
FM11   Colour fastness of household dyes
FM18   Surface tension and detergents
FM33   Assessment card

15.1
DISSOLVING OUT THE GREASE

Main idea in this section

'Dry cleaning' is a logical method of cleaning, but it may not be the most practical.

Applying
knowledge

Assessing
(relevant
factors)

It is worth considering dry cleaning first. The idea of dissolving the grease and hence removing the dust which accompanies it follows easily from Chapter 14. A satisfactory solvent must be non-toxic, non-flammable, and relatively inexpensive. Unfortunately all organic solvents tend to be expensive and if allowed to vaporize (like steam from water) would make the process prohibitively expensive and a health hazard. Therefore dry cleaning equipment must include a solvent recovery unit which adds to its size and cost. A wide variety of organic solvents have been used in the past. The main solvents used now are *perchloroethylene* and Solvent 113 (trade name *Arklone*, made by ICI), although some others are still used. Remind pupils of the dry cleaning symbols (figure T15.1).

145

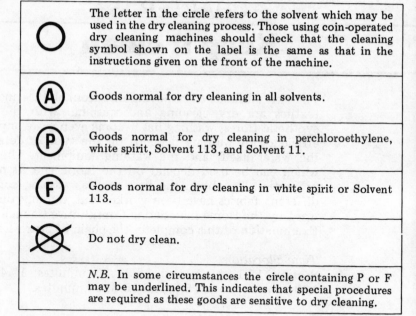

O	The letter in the circle refers to the solvent which may be used in the dry cleaning process. Those using coin-operated dry cleaning machines should check that the cleaning symbol shown on the label is the same as that in the instructions given on the front of the machine.
(A)	Goods normal for dry cleaning in all solvents.
(P)	Goods normal for dry cleaning in perchloroethylene, white spirit, Solvent 113, and Solvent 11.
(F)	Goods normal for dry cleaning in white spirit or Solvent 113.
⊗	Do not dry clean.
	N.B. In some circumstances the circle containing P or F may be underlined. This indicates that special procedures are required as these goods are sensitive to dry cleaning.

Figure T15.1
The dry cleaning symbols.

Figure 15.1
This photograph of a dry cleaner's emphasizes that dry cleaning equipment needs special provision.

15.2
WATER: CHEAP BUT INEFFICIENT

Main ideas in this section

Water has shortcomings as a cleaning agent.

If water alone would dissolve grease, the detergent industry would never have developed.

Figure 15.2

Observing

Communicating
(speech)

This illustrates the inefficiency of water. It is true that high temperatures and agitation may remove some grease using water alone, for instance when washing up under running water with a lot of rubbing, but there is a limit to its effectiveness particularly when grease and dirt have penetrated into the fibres in the fabric (unlike a plate where the grease is on the surface).

15.3
MAKING WATER WORK

Main idea in this section

Detergents break down the surface tension of water and assist in removing grease from fabrics.

Figures 15.3, 15.4, and 15.5
These show the initial stage of wetting the fabric, the structure of the detergent molecule, and the sequence of grease removal from the fabric surface.

WASHING WITH AND WITHOUT DETERGENT

Practical skills

You will need for each pair or group of pupils
Cotton fabric (2 pieces)   Detergent
Sewing machine oil   Stopwatch or clock

Assessing (validity)
Water as hot as the hand can comfortably withstand

Observing
Very light machine oil may be removed using hot water alone. Ensure that the oil soaks into the fabric, or use a heavier grade

Designing tests
oil such as motor oil. Remind the pupils to rub each sample for exactly the same time (about 30 seconds) and to use similar washing techniques (preferably light agitation to simulate the action of a washing machine).

Q 1
Evaluating
Although some of the oil may be removed by water alone, the presence of a detergent should produce a better result.

15.4
SOAP OR DETERGENT?

Main ideas in this section

Soap is derived from animal or vegetable fats and oils which are treated with caustic soda.

Soapless or synthetic detergents are built up from simple organic compounds largely derived from oil.

The difference between various soaps is mainly cosmetic.

Detergent powders, both soap and soapless, may contain a variety of substances in addition to the detergent itself.

15.5
WHAT IS IN WATER?

Main ideas in this section

Certain salts dissolved in the water cause it to be hard.

Soaps do not work very well in hard water, but soapless detergents are not affected by hardness.

Water softeners can be added to the water.

Link with school science
The water cycle is dealt with in science lessons in the first years of secondary school.

Figures 15.6 and 15.7
These show two stages in the cycle: a reservoir and a waterworks. Pure water is very difficult to obtain. Something is nearly always dissolved in it, including air (which allows fish to survive) and various salts.

Q 2

Reasoning logically

Since the salts are dissolved in the water, one way to remove them would be to boil the water. The water would form steam and evaporate, leaving the salts behind. The steam would have to be collected and cooled to form water.

Assessing (relevant factors)

The reason why the dissolved salts in the mains water are not treated in this way in Britain is that the energy cost of boiling off so much water is huge.

Extension work

Communicating (speech)

If you wish to demonstrate this, dissolve some common salt (sodium chloride) in a small amount of water, put the solution into a small saucepan and boil off the water. The salt will remain deposited at the bottom of the pan. Hold a cooled saucepan lid or ovenproof plate in the steam (remember to use oven gloves). Pure water will collect on it. ⚠

Link with school science
In most schools, pupils study water hardness in about the fourth year. The distribution of hard water can be related to the limestone or chalk in the rocks and linked with geography lessons as well.

Reasoning logically

Temporary hardness is caused by soluble bicarbonates of calcium and magnesium. When this water is boiled, the bicarbonate decomposes and forms insoluble carbonates. These are seen as the fur or scale on kettles and are deposited in hot water pipes, leading eventually to blockages (*figure 15.8*). Boiling has the effect of softening the water, hence the term temporary hardness.

Permanent hardness is caused by salts such as calcium and magnesium sulphate. These are unaffected by heat and so are not removed by boiling.

HOW HARD IS THE WATER?

You will need for each pair or group of pupils

Distilled water	3 boiling-tubes and corks
Tap water	Dropper
Hard water	Measuring cylinder
Soap solution	Stopwatch or clock

Practical
skills

Estimating

Measuring

Communicating
(writing and
maths)

The different types of water must all be at the same temperature. Distilled water can be obtained from the science laboratory or a garage. Hard water can be made up by adding 2 g calcium chloride to 1000 ml distilled water. The best soap solution to use is Wanklyn which can be obtained from a pharmacist's or is generally held by the science laboratory. Dilute Wanklyn soap solution in the ratio of 1 part soap solution to 3 parts water, as this gives clearer results. A dropper is easy to use for adding the soap solution. Alternatively, a more accurate result is obtained using a burette.

Q 3
The answer will depend on the tap water used.

HARD ON SOAP ...

Applying
knowledge

Soap combines with calcium and magnesium salts to form a scum which is a compound of calcium and magnesium with the soap. The calcium and magnesium salts therefore use up the soap, and until this reaction is complete no soap is available for washing. Contrary to popular belief, the scum which forms on a bath in hard water areas is not entirely from the person who is bathing, but also comes from the water.

NOT SO HARD ON DETERGENTS

Reasoning
logically

No chemicals in the composition of a soapless detergent react with calcium or magnesium salts and therefore no scum is formed.

WATER SOFTENERS

Applying
knowledge

Over the years, ways have been found to overcome water hardness. Some involve treatment of the whole water supply in the home, although the salts which are added in the process make the water less suitable for drinking. Water softeners such as bath salts can also be added on particular occasions. Some detergents contain water softeners.

WHAT IS THE EFFECT OF A WATER SOFTENER?

You will need for each pair or group of pupils

Hard water sample   Boiling-tubes and dropper
Soap solution   Measuring cylinder
Water softener   Stopwatch or clock

Use the hard water sample and the soap solution made up for the previous investigation. Two water softeners may be used: the sodium sesquicarbonate obtainable from the science laboratory or any proprietary water softener such as Radox, or a proprietary brand such as Calgon. There is a difference between the two. Sodium sesquicarbonate softens water by precipitating the calcium salts. This is seen as a cloudiness in the water. Calgon (sodium hexametaphosphate) softens water by linking with the calcium salts in such a way that the calcium is not available to react with the soap. It remains in solution so no scum is formed.

Q 4

The answer is yes. Less soap solution will be needed to produce a lather when a water softener has been added.

15.6
GETTING IT CLEAN

Main ideas in this section

Effective washing depends on the water, the detergent, the degree of heating, and the means of agitation.

Rinsing is needed to complete the process.

Modern detergent powders are not simply soap or synthetic detergents. They are a mixture of compounds, each designed to do a particular task. For example, the formulation includes a water softener. It will also contain an agent to prevent re-deposition of soil, a mild bleaching agent, ingredients to ensure that the powder is free-flowing, lather improvers (to stabilize the lather), and fluorescers which give the 'whiter than white' effect.

All detergent actions are improved by higher temperatures. In particular, the mild bleach does not operate effectively below $60\,^{\circ}C$. However, powders containing enzymes need a period of operation below $60\,^{\circ}C$. Enzymes are important constituents of low temperature detergents.

Link with school science
Pupils are likely to have met detergency by the fourth year.

Applying
knowledge

The obvious highest temperature is boiling ($100\,^\circ$C). The non-biological detergents are at their most effective at this temperature, provided that the fabric will withstand it.

Assessing
(relevant
factors)

Developments in detergents are likely to be related to more effective washing at low temperatures. This has clear implications for energy conservation. Effective washing can therefore be related to water, detergent, means of heating, and means of agitation. Effective rinsing is needed to complete the process.

WASHING EQUIPMENT

Assessing
(relevant
factors)

Reasoning
logically

Encourage the pupils to see that all the basic requirements for washing are present in any washing method they can think of. What varies is the efficiency of each factor and the amount of labour required to do it. In this way one can progress from *figures 15.9* and *15.10* to the systems shown in *figures 15.11*, *15.12*, and *15.13*. What has changed is not the basic principles but the means of carrying them out.

15.7
BUT IT WON'T WORK FOR EVERYTHING

Main ideas in this section

Different types of fibres mean that a variety of washing conditions are needed.

Polyester may remain creased if it is washed at too high a temperature.

Remind the pupils that, from the point of view of washing efficiency, the best system would be to use a detergent at boiling-point, with maximum agitation, for a long time. But wool shrinks as a result of vigorous washing and agitation, dyestuffs may run, and polyester can crease at high temperatures. Pupils should be able to envisage the need for a care labelling scheme.

COMPARING THE EFFECT OF DIFFERENT WASHING METHODS ON POLYESTER FABRIC

You will need for each pair or group of pupils

2 pieces of polyester fabric	Saucepan
(30 cm $\times$ 30 cm)	Bowl
Detergent	Washing tongs
	Rubber gloves
	Access to cooker

When carrying out instruction *1*, make sure that the fabric is in a bowl large enough to eliminate the possibility of creasing.

When carrying out instruction 2, it is important to wring the fabric when hot.

Q 6
The property of polyester which is affecting performance is its ability to retain a crease or pleat.

In the second part of the experiment the fabric is boiled so it is at a temperature of approximately 100 °C. When the fabric is removed from the saucepan and wrung, creases are put into it at 100 °C. This is repeated when it is rinsed in hot water and wrung again, though this might be at a slightly lower temperature. Directly it is removed from the water it is cooling, so immediately after it is wrung it will be cooler and the creases will remain set.

In the first part of the experiment, the fabric only reaches approximately 50 °C. The method of rinsing cools it to room temperature before any crease or pleat is inserted in it. Therefore, even if any wrinkling occurs when it is lifted from the bowl, the temperature is too low for it to remain set.

Emphasize the compromise that is needed to obtain the best washing conditions for polyester. The most efficient cleaning is balanced against achieving the best minimum iron performance.

15.8
GETTING IT RIGHT IN PRACTICE

Main idea in this section

The care labelling scheme provides instructions on how to wash different fabrics satisfactorily.

The Home Laundering Consultative Council scheme, now the International Textile Care Labelling Code since it was adopted in other European countries, is widely known. But the relationship between fabric type and conditions for each numbered process can only be understood by reference to the fibre and fabric performance properties and wash processing conditions.

Wash Code 1
Maximum wash conditions giving optimum cleaning are possible because cotton and linen retain durability in water, white fabrics have no dyestuff problems and there is no need to preserve minimum iron properties as there are none to preserve.

Wash Code 2
Exactly the same conditions as Wash Code 1 except the temperature is dropped to accommodate colours. Also viscose is included, even if white, as it is weaker in water and would be seriously weakened if boiled.

Wash Code 3
Nylon and polyester/cotton fabrics have no durability problems in washing, but the medium wash, lower temperature, and cold rinse with no wringing are designed to preserve minimum iron properties. Ideally this would require 50 °C but for white fabrics 60 °C is used to improve the whiteness.

Wash Code 4
A repeat of Wash Code 3 specifically designed for the general run of minimum iron fabrics. The special finishes referred to for cotton and viscose are the resin treatments (see Chapter 12).

Wash Code 5
A repeat of Wash Code 1 and 2 except that the temperature is lowered to 40 °C to accommodate poor dye fastness.

Wash Code 6
Essentially a repeat of Wash Code 4 aimed at preserving minimum iron properties but for fabrics which require more careful handling, *e.g.* wool blends, to ensure that the wool does not shrink, and acrylics, which tend to 'bag' at higher temperatures.

Wash Code 7
Similar to Wash Code 4 except that it is used for fabrics where minimum iron properties are not involved, so there is no need to rinse in cold water and a longer spin can be given.

Wash Code 8
About the most gentle machine wash possible for delicate fabrics with poor colour fastness.

Wash Code 9
A special programme put in for the German market when the H.L.C.C. went European. It is virtually unused in this country (and also now in Germany). It applied to resin-treated cotton which was so effective that it could be boiled and still retain its minimum iron properties. Unfortunately the durability problem was even worse than usual, hence the minimum wash and no spinning.

Evaluating   Finally, the garments have now come to the end of the chain. The theme which has run throughout the book of aesthetics, performance, and price should be re-emphasized in the final stages. One of the factors which influenced the initial choice will change and become unacceptable. When that happens the consumer can exercise his or her right to choose whether to buy another garment from the same source or go elsewhere and thus start the chain again.

Concepts and skills	Pupils may be able to:
15.1 *Dissolving out the grease* Detergency. Emulsification. *Science/maths* Detergency. Solvents. Properties of materials. Observing, Applying knowledge, Communicating (writing and speech), Assessing (relevant factors).	Explain how dry cleaning works. Explain the differences between the various dry cleaning symbols. Explain why dry cleaning is a relatively expensive process (the cost of materials and labour intensiveness).
15.2 *Water: cheap but inefficient* and **15.3** *Making water work* Detergency. Emulsification. *Science/maths* Detergency. Applying knowledge, Communicating (writing and speech), Practical skills, Assessing (validity), Designing tests.	Explain that water alone will not dissolve grease due to surface tension problems. Explain with diagrams the cleaning action of detergents. Suggest factors affecting their efficient use such as concentration of detergent; time/temperature/agitation relationship.
15.4 *Soap or detergent?* and **15.5** *What is in water?* Detergency. Hardness of water. Effective cleaning. *Science/maths* Detergency. Salts. Hardness of water. Reasoning logically, Assessing (relevant factors), Communicating (diagrams), Applying knowledge, Practical skills.	Define detergent as a substance which helps to remove dirt. Explain that in hard water dissolved calcium and magnesium salts react with the soap, limiting the cleaning action. Suggest reasons why soap products are bought even by people in hard water areas, such as local custom, development of modified products combining soap plus water softener.

Concepts and skills	Pupils may be able to:
15.6 *Getting it clean* **15.7** *But it won't work for everything* and **15.8** *Getting it right in practice* Washing processes. *Science/maths* Detergency. Time/temperature relationship. Properties of materials. Reasoning logically, Applying knowledge, Assessing (relevant factors), Practical skills, Classifying.	State correctly the factors necessary for effective cleaning, *i.e.* water, detergent, temperature, agitation, container. Discuss factors affecting cleaning such as temperature, time, agitation, rinsing, drying. Explain the importance of following different washing procedures for different fabrics (refer to HLCC code) and give some examples.

Idea for homework
The Background reading for this chapter is intended to draw pupils' attention to the size of the advertising industry and its power. How many advertisements do pupils see each week? Do they think they are affected by them? Do advertisements provide useful information? Discuss these ideas with pupils.

Reference material

British Man-Made Fibres Federation (1978) *Guide to man-made fibres.*

British Standards Institution, *British standards and textiles.* PP777.

Collier, A.M. (1974) *A handbook of textiles.* Pergamon.

Corbman, B.P. (1975) *Textiles: fibre to fabric.* McGraw-Hill.

Dyer, A. (1976) *Dyes from natural sources.* Bell & Hyman Ltd.

Dylon International Ltd. (Leaflets on various types of dyeing.)

Farnfield, C.A., and Alvey, P.J. (eds.) (1975) *Textile terms and definitions.* 7th edition. Textile Institute.

Farnfield, C.A., and Perry, D.R. (eds.) (1975) *Identification of textile materials.* Textile Institute.

Farnfield, C.A. (ed.) (1974) *A guide to sources of information in the textile industry.* Textile Institute.

Gale, E. (1971) *From fibres to fabrics.* Bell & Hyman Ltd.

Giles, C. (1974) *A laboratory course in dyeing.* S.D.C.

Hall, A.J. (1970) *The standard handbook of textiles.* 8th edition. Textile Book Service.

Hern, M.J. (1981) *The second skin.* 3rd edition. Houghton Mifflin Co.

Hollen, N., and Saddler, J. (1973) *Textiles.* Macmillan.

Home Laundering Consultative Council. *The international textile care labelling code: what it means to you.* (Free leaflet.)

Joseph, M. *Introductory textile science.* (1981) Holt, Rinehart & Winston.

Marks, R., and Robinson, A.T.C. (1976) *Principles of weaving.* Textile Institute.

Marks, R., and Robinson, A.T.C. (1973) *Woven cloth construction.* Textile Institute.

Nottingham Educational Supplies, 17 Ludlow Hill Road, Melton Road, West Bridgford, Nottingham NG2 6HD. Telephone 0602 234251. For materials pack to complement the study of fibres and fabrics.

Nuffield Combined Science (1980) Themes for the Middle Years: *Clothes* and *Colour.* Longman.

Nuffield Working with Science (1978) *Feet and footwear.* Longman Group Ltd, Resources Unit.

Nuffield Working with Science (1977) *Fibres and fabrics.* Longman Group Ltd, Resources Unit.

Nuffield Revised Chemistry (1976) *Option 10. Historical Topics.* Longman Group Ltd, Resources Unit. (See Section B, an outline history of the development of dyeing, both natural and synthetic.)

Nuffield Science 13 to 16 (1980) *Making molecules work for us* and *Chemical giants.* Longman Group Ltd, Resources Unit.

Nuffield Revised Chemistry (1978) *Teachers' guide III*. Longman. (See Option 10, Section B.)

Rees, A.M. (1976) *Experiments in home economics. Part 1, Textile science*. Blackwell.

Ridley, A., and Williams, D. (1974) *Simple experiments in textile science*. Heinemann Educational Books.

Robinson, S., and Wickens, H. *Dyes and dyeing*. 35 mm colour filmstrip. Griffin & George Ltd.

Seagroat, M. (1975) *Basic textile book*. Herbert Press.

Scott, G. (1977) *Transfer printing onto man-made fibres*. Batsford.

Smirfitt, J. (1975) *Introduction to weft knitting*. Merrow.

Storey, J. (1974) *Manual of textile printing*. Thames and Hudson.

Swaine, P. (1980) *Cleaning today*. Education unit, Lever Brothers Ltd.

Taylor, J. (1979) Science at work series. *Dyes and dyeing*. Addison-Wesley.

Thomas, D. (1971) *Introduction to warp knitting*. Merrow.

Thorn Domestic Appliances (Electrical) Ltd. (Catalogues of washing machines.)

Trotman, E.R. (1975) *Dyeing and chemical technology of textile fibres*. Griffin.

Unilever Education Section. (Booklets on *Detergents, Surface activity, Theory of detergency, Vegetables oils and fats*, and *Water*.)

Welford, T. (1969) *The textiles student's manual*. Pitman.

Useful addresses

Names and addresses of organizations which provide educational material, for some of which a charge is made.

Advertising Association, Abford House, 15 Wilton Road, London SW1V 1NJ.

Blackwell Scientific Publications Ltd (publishers of the *Journal of consumer studies and home economics*), Osney Mead, Oxford OX2 0EL.

British Gas Education Service, Room 414, 326 High Holborn, London WC1 7PT.

British Wool Marketing Board, Oak Mills, Clayton, Bradford, West Yorkshire BD14 6JD.

Consortium of Local Education Authorities for the Provision of Science Equipment (CLEAPSE), Brunel University, Uxbridge UB8 3PH.

Consumers' Association (publishers of *Which?*), 14 Buckingham Street, London WC2N 6DS.

Crafts Council, 12 Waterloo Place, London SW1V 4AU.

Design Council, The Design Centre, 28 Haymarket, London SW1Y 4SU.

Dylon International Ltd, Consumer Advice Bureau, Worsley Bridge Road, London SE26 5HD.

Electrical Association for Women, 25 Foubert's Place, London W1V 2AL.

Electricity Council, Understanding Electricity, 30 Millbank, London SW1P 4RD.

Griffin & George Ltd, 285 Ealing Road, Alperton, Wembley, Middlesex HA0 1HJ.

The home economist, Stonebridge Press, 823–825 Bath Road, Bristol BS4 5NU.

Home Laundering Consultative Council, c/o Clothing and Footwear Institute, Albert Road, Hendon, London NW4 2JS.

Modus, National Association of Teachers of Home Economics, Hamilton House, Mabledon Place, London WC1 9BJ.

ICI Fibres, 68 Knightsbridge, London SW1X 7LN.

International Institute for Cotton, Kingston Road, Didsbury, Manchester M20 8RD.

International Wool Secretariat, Wool House, Carlton Gardens, London SW1Y 5AE.

Journal of consumer studies and home economics, Blackwell Scientific Publications Ltd, Osney Mead, Oxford OX2 0EL.

Lever Brothers Education Unit, International Teaching Resource Centre, PO Box 10, Wetherby, Yorkshire LS23 7EH.

Longman Group Ltd, Longman House, Burnt Mill, Harlow, Essex CM20 2JE.

Longman Resources Unit, 33—35 Tanner Row, York YO1 1JP.
Marks and Spencer Ltd, Michael House, 47—67 Baker Street, London W1A 1DN.
Nottingham Educational Supplies, 17 Ludlow Hill Road, Melton Road, West Bridgford, Nottingham NG2 6HD.
Office of Fair Trading, Field House, Breams Buildings, London EC4.
Philip Harris Ltd, Lynn Lane, Shenstone, Staffordshire WS14 0EE.
Royal Society for the Prevention of Accidents, Cannon House, The Priory, Queensway, Birmingham B4 6BS.
Shirley Institute, Didsbury, Manchester M20 8RX.
Silk Educational Service, 37 Chinbrook Road, Grove Park, London SE12 9TQ.
Stonebridge Press (publishers of *The home economist*), 823—825 Bath Road, Bristol BS4 5NU.
Textile Institute, 10 Blackfriars Street, Manchester M3 5DR.
Thorn Domestic Appliances (Electrical) Ltd, New Lane, Havant, Hampshire PO9 2NH.
Tropical Products Institute, 56—62 Gray's Inn Road, London WC1X 8LU.
Unilever Education Section, PO Box 68, Unilever House, London EC4P 4BQ.
Unilever Films, Scottish Central Film Library, 74 Victoria Crescent Road, Glasgow G12 9JN.

Index

A

abrasion, 74-5
acetate, 38, 43, 45, 56, 58, 75, 93
acrylic, 38, 39, 43, 45, 56, 59, 60, 75-6, 93, 128
adhesives, 102
aesthetic factors, 1-10, 11, 15-16, 21, 27, 28, 29, 31, 34, 36, 43, 44, 45, 58, 70, 71, 73-4, 86, 89, 93, 94, 103, 124-5
air-jet process, 93, 138
alginate, 36
Angora hair fibre, 35
animal skins, 24, 25-7
anoraks, 81, 83-4, 131
anti-static fabrics, 70, 81

B

bed linen, 21
bleaching, 124
blended fabrics, 84-5
block printing, 117
boll weevil, 49
bonded-fibre fabrics, 102, 103
brand names, 37-40, 46
brushing, 124, 125, 129

C

calendering, 124, 129
Calico Printers, Lancashire, 37, 59
camel hair fibres, 35
Carothers, Dr Wallace, 59
cellulose, 36, 54, 57-8, 110
chain of trade, 19-20, 23
chain stores, 7, 20
Chardonnet, Count Hilaire, 57
cleaning fabrics, 124, 129, 145-55
clothes, 70; shopping for, 1-10; social customs and climatic conditions, 12-13; see also garments
coats, fur and sheepskin v. woollen textile, 26
colour, 106-12; see also dyeing; printing
compromises, 8-10, 127, 130, 151-2
conduction, 82, 83

consumers, 1, 4; and suppliers, 6-7, 9
continental quilts, 20
convection, 82, 83, 84
cotton, 21, 29, 36, 41-2, 43, 44, 45, 48-9, 50-1, 54, 58, 61, 63, 73, 75, 78, 90, 154; dyeing, 109-10; pests (boll weevil), 49; polyester blended with, 85, 127, 153; resin-treated, 125-7, 144; spinning, 91; thread, 137-8
Cotton Institute, 40
Courtaulds, 38, 58, 63
creasing and wrinkling, 76-8, 126
crimp, 50, 63, 90; gear, 93
Crimplene, 38, 93
crocodile skins, 26
Cross and Bevan, 57-8
cross-dyeing, 116

D

denim jeans, 44
department stores, 20
detergents, 144, 145, 147, 149, 150, 154
direct mail order, 20
dirt, getting dirty, 141-4; see also washing
distaff spindle, 91
distributive trades, 20
dobby looms, 100
drape of fabrics, 15-16, 31, 103, 135
drip-dry fabrics, 79
dry cleaning, 124, 145-6
Du Pont Co, U.S.A., 59
durability, 27, 29, 30-1, 32, 70, 72, 74-6, 85, 86, 138, 152; chemical breakdown, 75; physical factors, 74-5
dyestuffs, dyeing, 19, 106, 108-17, 122; absorption spectra, 108, 110-11; combining, 111; commercial practice, 113-14; cross-dyeing, 116; direct and vat, 110; disperse, 110; fast colours, 72, 108, 109;

melt or polymer, 115; piece dyeing, 116; synthetic 110; see also printing

E

E.E.C. regulations, 39
elastane fabrics, 101
Elmendorf Tear Strength Tester, 127

F

fabrics, 13, 20; blended, 84-5; bonded fibre, 102, 103; cling, 70; comparison of properties, 70-84; dirty 141-4; drape, 15-16; dry cleaning, 145-6; dyed, 63-4, 106, 108-10, 114-17; finishing, 123-34; foam backed, 14; grey or greige, 124; handling tests, 15-16; knitted, 100-2; labels, 40, 84, 152; nonwoven, 24, 97, 102-3, 105; patterned, 100, 106, 114, 117-22; producing from yarn, 89, 97-105; producing garments from, 132-40; production processes, 24-5, 32; sett/set, 99; stitch-bonded, 102-3; strength, 29-31, 70; stretch, 101-2; tear strength, 30-1; washing, 146-55; woven, 93, 97-100, 101-2, 103, 104; see also cotton; fibres; garments; wool
false twist process, 93
fashion, 21, 44
fashion designers/design, 133, 140
felt, 76, 102
felting, 76
fibres, 17-18, 24, 31, 34-47; blending, 70, 84-5; burning tests to identify, 64, 67; classifying, 36;

comparison of properties, 70-84; cotton, 36, 41-2, 45, 48-9, 50-1, 54; crimp, 50, 63; definition, 34-5; dyeing, 108, 110, 113-14, 115-16,117; examining, 18-19; filament, 52, 53, 62-3; generic v. brand names, 37-40, 46; identifying different, 63-7, 69; linen, 49-50; man-made, 35, 36, 39, 40, 41, 42-3, 54, 55-63; microscopic examination, 65-6, 67; natural, 35-6, 37, 40, 41, 43, 48-55; price, 43-5; producing yarn from, 89-95; regenerated, 36, 57-8; silk, 35, 43, 44, 45, 52-4; spun, 61; staple, 17, 48, 50, 53, 62, 63; synthetic, 28, 35, 36, 42-3, 44, 47, 56, 59-60; variation in lengths, 50-1, 92; wool, 36, 40, 43, 45, 48, 49, 50-1, 54

filament yarn/fibres, 13, 52, 62-3, 92, 93; flat, 92-4, 95-6; mono-, 52, 53; multi-, 17, 52, 53, 63, 125

finishing, 24, 25, 76, 123-31; functional, 123; resin-treated cotton, 125-7; routine, 124

flammability, 7, 64, 70, 72, 75, 137

Fortrel, 39

'fullness', putting in, 134-5

G

garments, 11-18, 132-40; breaking down, 13-18, 22-3; dirty, 141-4; dry cleaning, 145-6; dyeing, 15; engineering the shape, 132-5; joining up, 135; labelling, 37, 40, 84, 145, 152; making from different materials, 28-9; putting in 'fullness', 134-5; seams, 136, 137; threads, 14, 137-8; trimmings, 13, 14, 115, 138; washing, 146-55; waterproof, 123, 128, 130-1; see also clothes; fabrics

gear crimp, 93

generic v. brand names, 37-40, 46

glue, 89, 135

grease, grease stains, 142, 143, 145, 146

H

handle of fabrics, 15-16, 31 103, 124, 135

heat retention see thermal insulation

H.L.C.C. labelling, 145, 152

hosiery and stocking manufacture, 100

household textiles, 12, 20-1

hydrophilic fibres, 79, 87

hydrophobic fibres, 79, 81, 87, 144

I

ICI, 37-9, 93

insulation, 81-4, 87

interlacing (yarn), 16-17, 97-8, 104

interlinings, 13-14, 17, 26, 102, 103

interlock fabrics, 100

International Textile Care Labelling Code, 152

International Wool Secretariat, 40, 128

J

Jacquard looms, 100

J-cloths, 103

jersey fabric, 38, 73, 100, 124; double, 93, 100

joining up garments, 135

K

kagouls, 131

knit-de-knit process, 93

knitting, knitwear, 13, 100-2, 104; dyeing, 115

knitting machines, 100-1; circular, 100

knife edge process, 93

L

labelling, 37, 40, 84, 152

linen, 49-50, 152

linings, 17, 26

lock stitch, 136

looms, 100

M

machinery, cost of, 25

mail order catalogues, 20

man-made fibres, 35, 36, 39, 40, 41, 42, 52, 54, 56-63, 114; blended, 50-1; generic v. brand names, 37-40; regenerated, 36, 57-8; spinning, 92; synthetic, 28, 35, 36, 42-3, 44, 47, 56, 59-60

market stalls, 20

Merino sheep, 51

mohair, 35

molecules, 17, 18, 19, 54, 58, 61, 75

moulding, 133-4

N

natural fibres, 35-6, 37, 40, 41, 43, 48-55, 56, 92; blended with man-made fibres, 50-1

nonwoven fabrics, 24, 97, 102-3, 105

nylon, 38, 43, 45, 56, 59, 60, 63, 75, 78, 79, 81, 83, 84, 125, 153; brushed, 125; warp-knit, 125

O

oil, 43, 44, 59

overlock stitch, 13, 136

P

pants, paper v. cotton, 30-1

paper see plastics and paper

party plan, 20

patterns, patterned fabric, 100, 106, 114, 116

perchloroethylene, 145

performance factors, 1-10, 11, 21, 28, 29, 30-1, 34, 40, 44, 45, 58, 70, 71, 86, 89, 125

photosynthesis, 54

piece dyeing, 116

piece goods, 20

plastic chips, 28

plastic macs, 30

plastics and paper, 24-32

pleat retention, 78-9

polyester, 28, 37-8, 39, 42, 43, 45, 56, 59, 60, 63, 75, 78, 81, 82, 102, 103; blended, 85, 153; dyeing, 109-10; spun and texturized, 92, 93, 94; thread, 137-8; washing, 151-2, 153

polymers, 54, 56, 61, 68, 81, 114, 126; regenerating natural, 57-8, 68; synthetic, 59-60, 68, 115
polypropylene, 29
polythene, 29, 33
price, price factors, 1-10, 11, 21, 25, 26-7, 28, 29, 31, 34, 43-5, 58, 85
printing, printed fabrics, 19, 106, 113, 114, 117-22; block, 117; roller, 117-18, 120; screen, 118, 120; transfer, 119, 121-2; see also dyeing
production costs, 43-5, 54
protective clothing, 131
proteins, 54

R
'rag trade', 19
raincoats, 128, 130, 131; plastic macs, 30
raw materials, cost of, 26, 28
regenerated fibres, 36, 57-8
resin-treated cotton, 125-7 130, 144
retailers, retailing, 7, 20
roller printing, 117-18, 120

S
Sarille, 63
Schappé systems, 92, 138
screen printing, 118, 120
seams, 136; overlock, 13, 136; stretch properties, 136, 137-8; unpicking, 13
shape retention, 70, 72, 76-9, 86
sheep, 51
sheepskin coats, 26
sheets, fitted, 20
shopping, 1-10
shrinkage, shrinking, 76, 128
silicone-treated fabrics, 128, 130
silk, silkworm, 35, 43, 44, 45, 48, 52-4, 55, 56, 57, 75, 93; flat filament, 93; spun, 92
Silk Institute, 40
sisal, 35-6
size retention, 70, 72, 137
skins and furs, 13, 24, 25-7, 32
slippage, 99
soap, 147, 149
solvents, 145-6

spinning, spun yarn, 63, 91-2, 94, 95-6
staple fibres, 17-18, 48, 50, 53, 62, 63, 92, 93, 94, 138
static electricity, 80-1, 87, 144
stentering, 124, 129
stitch-bonded fabrics, 102-3
stretch, 101-2; of seams, 136
stuffer box process, 93
Sulzer loom, 100
sunlight, effect of, 75
suppliers and consumers, 6-7, 9
synthetic fibres, 28, 35, 36, 42-3, 44, 47, 56, 59-60, 61, 62, 63, 65, 77, 79, 80, 81, 84, 93, 115, 126, 144, 145

T
tailors, 134
Taslan, 93
tear strengths of materials, 30-1, 127
tearing, 75
tensile action (pulling), 75
technology and science, 7, 9
tent fabric, 73
tentering, 124, 129
Terylene, 37-8
textile testing industry, 88
textiles, 11, 20, 55, 70, 71; application of colour to, 108-12; chain of trade, 19-20; characteristic properties, 15, 22; drape and distortion, 15-16; fabric production processes, 24-5; going shopping for, 1-10; household, 12, 20-1; industrial uses, 12; labels, 37, 40, 84; plastics and paper v., 25-7; variety, 11-13, 22; see also fabrics
texturized yarns, 92, 93-4, 95-6
thermal insulation, 70, 72, 81-4
threads, 14, 137-8
'throwing', 93
towelling, 73
transfer printing, 119, triacetate, 38, 43, 45, 56, 58, 75
trimmings, 13, 14, 115, 138
twist, 91, 92, 95; false, 93

U
underwear, 73; paper pants, 30-1; thermal, 82

V
velvet, 73
vicuna, 36
viscose, 36, 38, 43, 44, 45, 56, 57-8, 63, 64, 75, 93, 102, 152; blended, 85
Viyella, 37

W
warp, 98, 100, 115-16
warp-knitting, 100, 101-2, 125
'washability', 72
washing, 145, 146-55; care labelling scheme, 152-3; equipment, 151; with detergents, 147, 150-1
water, 147-50; absorption, 70, 72, 79-80; hard, 148, 149; rinsing, 150; softeners, 149-50
water-proofing, 123, 128, 130-1
weaving, woven fabrics, 93, 97-100, 101-1, 103, 104, 105
weft ('filling'), 98, 100, 115-16
weft-knitting, 100-2
Whinfield and Dickson, 59
wholesalers, 20
wool, 36, 40, 41, 42, 43, 44, 45, 48, 49, 50-1, 54, 72, 73, 75, 76, 90, 124; blended with viscose, 85; crimp in, 50; finishing processes, 124, 128; reclaimed, 40; shrinkage, 128; spinning, 91-2; Superwash, 70, 81, 123; textile coats, 26; thermal insulation, 81, 82; worsted yarn, 91-2, 123
worsted, 91, 123

X
X-ray diffraction, 19

Y
yarn, 16-17, 24, 25, 52, 63, 89-105; combed, 92; conversion to fabric, 97-105; dyeing, 114, 115-16, 117; fancy and exotic, 94, 96; filament, 13, 17, 52, 53, 63, 92-3;

162

arn (continued)
  flat filament, 92-4, 95-6;
  interlaced, 16-17, 97;
  producing from fibres,
  89-96; properties, 71;
  putting twist into, 91, 92;
  spun, 91-2, 94, 95-6; staple,
  63; texturized, 38, 92,
  93-4, 95-6; woven, 93,
  97-100

Z
zig-zag stitch, 136